THE JUBILEE GOSPEL

THE JUBILEE GOSPEL

The Jubilee, Spirit and the Church

Kim Tan

Authentic

MILTON KEYNES ● COLORADO SPRINGS ● HYDERABAD

14 13 12 11 10 09 08   7 6 5 4 3 2 1

First published in 2008 by Authentic Media
9 Holdom Avenue, Bletchley, Milton Keynes, Bucks, MK1 1QR
1820 Jet Stream Drive, Colorado Springs, CO 80921, USA
Medchal Road, Jeedimetla Village, Secunderabad 500 055, A.P., India
www.authenticmedia.co.uk
Authentic Media is a division of IBS-STL U.K., limited by guarantee, with its
Registered Office at Kingstown Broadway, Carlisle, Cumbria, CA3 0HA.
Registered in England & Wales No. 1216232. Registered charity 27016

British Library Cataloguing in Publication Data

A catalogue record for this book is available from
the British Library.

ISBN-13: 978-1-86024-703-3

Cover Design by Rachel Myatt
Print Management by Adare
Printed in Great Britain by J.H. Haynes and Co., Sparkford

Contents

Acknowledgements

We all know the excitement of discovering something new. We want to share it with everyone, because we think they haven't seen what we have. Imagine then my disbelief when some years later I met some Mennonites, a 450-year-old branch within the Anabaptist tradition, only to discover that they have been teaching and practising Jubilee for a few hundred years! One of those I met was Dr Alan Kreider, who has become a friend and teacher. From him, I learnt much about social holiness and the common life of the Mennonites. He introduced me to the Anabaptist literature including doctoral theses on Jesus and the Jubilee. So what for me was 'new', was in fact very old. As old as the Laws of Moses.

A special 'thank you' is due to all the members of the Denzil Road Community, Guildford, UK. We radically and faithfully sought to practise what we had learnt about Jubilee during our time in community. We had our good times and our bad times but my life has been enriched, challenged and forever shaped by our economic-sharing and lifestyle as a family. I will always be grateful for that part of our history together. I have learnt much from conversation with many wonderful people over the years. There are too many to name here.

Daniel Cooling has done a magnificent job with the editing of the book. I am grateful.

Foreword by Mark Greene

A Whole Different Kind of World

It's 13 January 2006. London. LICC's offices.

Eighteen business people have gathered for '24' part 1, not, like Jack Bauer, to try to save the world in 24 hours, but rather to spend 24 hours thinking seriously about how to change their bit of it.

A venture capitalist is expounding the biblical teaching about Jubilee. His name is Kim Tan. What, you might well ask, have principles given to nomadic tribes some 3,000 years ago got to do with running twenty-first-century businesses, twenty-first-century communities or twenty-first-century families?

I had given Kim an hour and a half. After an hour and a quarter I could see that these 18 people are riveted. I am too. I give Kim an extra half hour. And then a further 45 minutes. I should have given him the rest of the day.

The impact is stunning.

One managing director had been wrestling with the question of how to sell his company – to whom and for whose benefit? The Jubilee principle of the generous distribution of wealth makes the critical difference to his decision to forego personal gain for the benefit of his wider team. Another entrepreneur is considering what principles should shape the culture of his rapidly-growing small business. Again, Kim's exposition of the Jubilee principles of generosity, rest and wholeness continue to radically impact the way he now leads that company.

The Jubilee Gospel, however, is not just about business, it is about a different vision for living all of life, a vision of generosity not accumulation, of relational richness not gated communities, of genuine hope for those who seem to have no opportunity to flourish. It's a blueprint for mercy, for justice, for *shalom*. It's a window into the heart of God, a lens through which to understand the kind of world that Jesus wants his people to work for.

It's a vision for a whole world.

And its values apply sharply to me and my family and my church, as well as to governments and their policies.

I've known Kim for well over a decade now and there are things he doesn't tell you in this book: things about how he and his family pursue the Jubilee way in every aspect of their life, about his own startling business success, about the sheer range of ways in which he has sought to serve the poor through business, about the time he has spent with governments on the behalf of the poor.

He would probably say that his story is not the main issue.

And it isn't.

Still, as you read this book, perhaps it is helpful to know that this scholar entrepreneur, this theologian venture capitalist, has not only thought deeply about the Jubilee Gospel, he's tried to live it out. And a lot of people round the world would say he's done a pretty good job. And a lot of people would say their lives have been changed for the better.

That's the potential this teaching has: not only to make a difference to your life but to help you make a difference to other people's.

May it be so.

Mark Greene, LICC
London, 2008

Foreword by Roger Forster

Kim Tan has done us a great service with his book on the Jubilee. It is a careful and comprehensive survey of the Jubilee Sabbath concept and its related subjects. His exposition is an inquiry into how Jesus understood and used this subject in his good news proclamation. It is an honour to write a foreword for this stimulating work. May many be reignited by the wonder of Christ's good news and his anointing Spirit as they read and know that same Spirit that enabled Jesus to proclaim the 'acceptable year of the Lord', namely the Jubilee. Here we may read and capture – or be captured by – the breadth, breath and excitement of the Jesus programme.

I had the privilege, some while ago, to address the workers, supporters and beneficiaries of an inner city Christian social action charity involved in a variety of regeneration, re-habitation and recovery services. I reminded them of how the work began in intensive prayer, made largely in our prayer-house by a small group of Jesus' followers who were excitedly committed to rediscover the message of Jesus in terms of the Old Testament Jubilee. One of the answers to these prayers was this particular charity and its commitment to the poor and disadvantaged in our needy city. In prayer and study we began to find Jubilee concepts all over the gospels and the Acts of the Apostles, or in other words, in all that Jesus began and continued to do and teach (Acts 1:1).

It has to be said that not all were as enthusiastic as those reported above. Perhaps it was thought to be too demanding. It is demanding, and Kim will bring this home to us as we proceed through his book. Perhaps I may be permitted another anecdote. I was a speaker some years ago in a conference on the subject of Christians serving as 'Salt and Light' in society. My own and other speakers' references to the Jubilee teaching evoked a somewhat disparaging remark from a fellow contributor; that we had squeezed every last drop of truth and teaching out of the brief mention of the Jubilee passage. However, I believe that any perceptive reader of Kim's exposition will find this Old Testament celebration of the fiftieth year a fundamental concept used by Jesus in the New Testament to establish the lifestyle to which he calls us. This sort of Christianity might be called 'Jubilee lifestyle Christianity'. By reading Kim's work one will come to see that this sort of Christianity is the norm, expected by Jesus, even if some practices may outwardly look different in a twenty-first century, international, urban context.

Leviticus 25 and other Old Testament passages concerned with sabbaths and Jubilees appear in the New Testament laying down basic Christian virtues and doctrines. The following are twelve prominent and representative subjects based in the Jubilee material. The reader will find Kim dealing with these in this book. These are clearly foundational to Christianity: forgiveness, release, debts, the poor, redistribution of wealth, sabbath rest, peace, faith, grace, atonement, inheritance, family; plus a thirteenth, the Trumpet (ram's horn equals Jubilee). All of these themes are found in the Gospels and Acts in such passages as Mt. 5:3,5; 6:12,14–15,31; Mk. 2:27,28; 3:33–35; Lk. 4:18,19; 23:34 (where 'forgive' means 'release'); Jn. 8:32; 11:52; Acts 2:44–46 and 4:32–35. These selections are just a few fairly obvious New Testament verses using the Jubilee themes and concepts but many other allusions may be found going back to this wonderful lifestyle enjoined upon God's people in the Old Testament.

Kim's work is clear, concise and challenging. It is presenting truth to be obeyed, not truth simply for intellectual information concerning the final great Jubilee sabbath rest of God. It is true that the writer of Hebrews speaks of a final sabbath rest remaining to the people of God (Heb. 4:11), and the need to press on into this future sabbath celebration. However, Kim also urges us to realise that 'future' in the present, as Jesus taught in Matthew 11:28–30 where the rest or 'sabbath' is a present experience for our souls. Our current experience of the Jubilee Gospel lifestyle, and our knowledge of the last trumpet (ram's horn) call of this age, will make us long for the consummation of the ages and a rich entrance into the final Jubilee of God.

This book will inspire us to further strive to enter richly into God's kingdom now, and in 'that great day'.

Roger Forster
January 2008

Preface

Over twenty years ago, my friend and teacher Roger Forster gave me a book by John Howard Yoder called *The Politics of Jesus*. Roger is a great reader of books but I had not seen him as excited about any particular book as this one. The short chapter in Yoder's book on the Jubilee was the catalyst that set me off on a journey through the Bible that resulted in turning my world upside down. And not just mine but many others' as well. The discovery of the Jubilee message led me and a small group of student friends to start a one-year experiment of economic sharing on our university campus. Pooling our grant money together, we lived on a minimal budget and gave the excess away to overseas students experiencing hardship due to the steep hike in UK tuition fees. We shared what we had. It was radical. It was exciting. We were young idealistic students wanting to live out our faith in a more radical and biblical way. Word quickly spread around the campus despite our efforts to keep it quiet, in case the experiment failed! It was clear that I was not a man of faith.

We so 'enjoyed' this communal lifestyle that we moved off campus following the graduation of a number of the group, and bought our first community house, again for another one-year experiment. We ended up with around forty of us in active community, living in twelve houses for eight years. To paraphrase early Christian theologian Tertullian, we had all things in common except our wives and our books! (Lending books to

Christians is one sure way of losing them.) We gave ourselves to intense studying of the Bible, discipleship and evangelism. Hundreds passed through, countless hungry students fed, many needs were met, lives touched and transformed. Heady times indeed.

Discovering the message of Jubilee reminded me of my early days, when as a young Christian I had felt the excitement of reading the early chapters of Acts. What an incredible picture of the early church sharing their lives together in radical expressions of love for one another. It was one of the key factors that attracted me to faith – the other being the person of Jesus that I discovered in the Gospels. But when I asked why the church was no longer like the one in Acts, mature Christians around me explained that God no longer worked in such radical and supernatural ways. Because we had the Bible, we supposedly no longer needed the Holy Spirit's power and manifestations for evangelism and holy living. And besides, a community lifestyle with economic sharing was not normal and the community in Jerusalem was a failed experiment. Who was I, a young Christian then, to challenge this kind of dispensational thinking as a cop out? It had the effect of putting me off the scent for a number of years, though all the while I retained an inner stirring of dissatisfaction about my own life and witness.

Reading Yoder's chapter on the Jubilee was the breath of fresh air I needed. I had begun to suspect that Christians could be remarkably adept at cooking up excuses for disobeying or disregarding the Bible – disingenuous even. Even those happy to be called 'evangelical' – and so in theory committed to the authority of the Christian Scriptures – can go to great lengths to explain away the full demands of the Bible in key areas of practice, perhaps because they cost and hurt too much to seem realistic. Yoder gave me the key to understanding the ministry of Jesus in Jubilee terms. From there it was a short hop to understanding Acts as the outworking of Jubilee for God's new people. Then a love affair with the Old Testament followed, particularly with the books of Leviticus, Deuteronomy and the Prophets, because I saw that Jubilee was intimately tied up with God's vision for the nation of Israel. As such, this is what *The Jubilee Gospel* is about – a tracing of the themes through the Bible that define the vision of Jubilee.

First, this is a book about *holiness* – not the contemplative and individualistic variety, but 'social holiness'.[1] When we think about holiness, we tend to think in terms of a personal holiness, often limited to our worship on Sundays, that is our spiritual life. This is because Western thought has long been influenced by Greek dualism which separates spirit and body, spiritual and material, sacred and secular. This has influenced our thinking to such an extent that our faith is regarded as a primarily personal and spiritual reality. Our faith, therefore, does not by definition affect our work, play, money and politics. However, in Hebrew thinking faith is all-embracing, touching every area of life. As we will see, Jubilee holiness touches every part of our lives.

Second, this book is about *economics* – God's style of economics. The kind of economics that would result in a society that reflects God's justice and compassion. The subject of the Jubilee raises the questions, 'What kind of a people are we supposed to be? How does God want his people to live?' The vision of the Jubilee answers that it is about being a holy nation that embraces kingdom economics and politics. It is about God's humanitarianism, God's justice and his vision of a just society. In this book we will not be dealing with 'spiritual' matters but will be talking about loans, interest rates, land ownership and social structures because, amongst other things, Jubilee touches our economic lives. The early chapters of Acts are more about holy economics than about spiritual gifts, as we shall see. The late Lesslie Newbigin rightly wrote: 'It is surely a fact of inexhaustible

---

[1] A term originally used by John Wesley, but popularised by Alan Kreider in his *Journey Towards Holiness: A Way of Living for God's Nation*.

significance that what our Lord left behind him was not a book, nor a creed, nor a system of thought, nor a rule of life, but a visible community' (*The Household of God*, SCM Press). Bishop Newbigin was correct. Jesus left behind a visible community in Acts so that the world could see what God is really like. Throughout the Old Testament, too, God was seeking to create a people who would truly reflect his character. At heart, God is seeking to build a Jubilee nation with kingdom economics.

Third, this book is about *biblical integrity* – belief and behaviour, creed and conduct, faith and works being integrated. Our faith has to touch the needs of our world – poverty, injustices and exploitation. The true test of our faith is our works. Risk-taking always accompanies faith. In fact someone has said that faith is spelt 'RISK'. Faith is not something we possess but something we practise.

Primarily, however, this book is about *following Jesus*. I came to faith because I was drawn to the personality of Jesus. Part of that attraction was his radical compassion, his holy defiance of the status quo, standing with the poor, the marginalised and teaching his followers to be peacemakers. This was a Jesus I had not heard much about in church but one I had started to discover through the Jubilee. It is a call to a faithful following of the Way.

Dr Kim Tan

1

The Nazareth Manifesto

Jesus' inaugural speech at the beginning of his ministry in Luke 4 set the scope and tenor for his life's work. A new president or prime minister taking office sets out his manifesto in an inaugural speech. Of the milestones in the life of Jesus, this was surely one of the greatest – his whole adult life had been geared towards this moment. How will Jesus describe his mission? How will he communicate his vision, his strategy and raise the expectations of a people under Roman occupation? A general going into battle has to have a clear strategy, he must choose the methods he will deploy to achieve his objectives.

Interestingly, Jesus chose the synagogue in his little hometown of Nazareth to launch his campaign and make his first speech. It was customary for the president of the synagogue to invite a distinguished person present to read the appointed passage of Old Testament scriptures and then speak. In the synagogue, it was customary to complete the reading of the *Torah* over 3 years. In addition, there was a second reading called the *haftarah* ('conclusion'). It consisted of portions from the Prophets and Writings related to the *Torah* reading for the week. So it was that Jesus was invited to give the *haftarah* reading from the scrolls of Isaiah 61:

> The Spirit of the Lord is on me,
>> because he has anointed me to preach good news to the poor.
> He has sent me to proclaim freedom for the prisoners

and recovery of sight for the blind,
to release the oppressed,
to proclaim the year of the Lord's favour.

After finishing reading the text, he sat down (as was the custom of the rabbis when they taught) and said, 'Today this scripture is fulfilled in your hearing,' and then the whole synagogue erupted into chaos. The audience was upset for a number of reasons. First, this was what would be accomplished by the Messiah when he came. Second, the reception of his inspiring words was mixed with scepticism about his origins. Here was this carpenter, known to all in the synagogue since he was a kid as Joseph's son, claiming to fulfil this messianic text. Third, using the stories of the widow of Zarephath and Naaman, Jesus implied that the promise from Isaiah would be fulfilled not among the Jews but the Gentiles. To the Jews who understood the text, this claim by Jesus was outrageous. To be told that the long-awaited blessings for Israel would in fact be more eagerly received among the Gentiles was an insult to the Jews. No wonder they drove him out of the town and tried to throw him off a cliff.

The Nazareth manifesto using Isaiah 61 was itself slightly unusual. Supposedly religious, it nevertheless had a strong political tone. It highlighted the role of the Spirit and spoke of healing, yet it contained language that would appeal to the freedom fighters seeking independence from the Roman conquerors. A strange mix then of religious as well as political objectives. The original perspective of Isaiah's prophecy was clearly one of deliverance from political oppression. Therefore in adopting this as his manifesto, Jesus intended his mission to be in line with Isaiah's vision. Clearly there were radical and revolutionary elements in this mission statement encompassing the political, economic, social as well as 'spiritual' spheres of life. It was to be a holistic mission to a broken world encompassing social holiness and justice. Compare this then to the often narrow understanding of mission that we have today, stemming largely from an interpretation of the Great Commission in Matthew 28. Here mission is frequently narrowly understood largely as evangelism and discipleship (plus baptism according to certain denominations). Should not the church be understanding terms such as 'discipleship' and 'evangelism' in light of Jesus' mission statement from Luke 4?

What does 'good news to the poor' mean? The 'good news' or 'gospel' is not the minimum requirement for entry into heaven as is largely understood today. The *euangelion* (good news) in Roman times referred to the news of a victory in battle or the coming of a new king. The good news that the Jews were expecting was the announcement of the coming of the Messiah who would bring in his kingdom, rebuild the temple and drive out the Roman occupation army. It was the kind of news that had an impact on people's lives on earth.

And what is 'the year of the Lord's favour'? Isaiah is referring to the failed programme of Jubilee which God had instituted for Israel to carry out when they entered the Promised Land. This was a radical socio-economic programme that would have resulted in social holiness for the nation. But it failed. It was never carried out by the nation of Israel. Why? Because it was too radical. The individual cost of obedience was too high for Israel. At the human level, given people's self-centeredness, it may even be regarded as impossible, a kind of utopian dream.

In announcing his ministry with the words from Isaiah 61, Jesus was in effect saying that the Jubilee programme may have failed in the Old Testament but it was by no means dead. God is still interested in a people characterised by social holiness, and Jesus and his disciples, through the Holy Spirit, were the agents for bringing this into being. Some scholars have calculated that AD 26–27 was an actual Jubilee year. Although this is unlikely,[1] it

---

[1] I. Howard Marshall, *The Gospel of Luke: A Commentary on the Greek Text*.

is possible that one was fresh in their minds from previous years. Even if some find this doubtful, it is clear that by the time of Jesus people understood Is. 58:6 and 61:1,2 as reinterpreting Lev. 25 so that the age of salvation would be the age of final Jubilee, of God's in-breaking reign.[2]

Against this background, the announcement that Jesus had come to usher in the Jubilee year is even more striking. We therefore have good reason to view the ministry of Jesus, and so the mission of the church, from the perspective of Jubilee. At the beginning of his ministry then, Jesus had gone to a failed programme in the Old Testament to use as his manifesto. He had come to introduce Jubilee.

---

[2] Joel Green, *The Theology of the Gospel of Luke.*

2

The Jubilee Programmes

So what was the Jubilee? It was the third of three radical economic programmes that God instituted for the nation of Israel:

- the tithing programme, every 3 years (Deut. 14:28; 26:12);
- the sabbath programme, every 7 years (Deut. 15; Lev. 25);
- the Jubilee programme, every 50 years (Lev. 25).

We will collectively call these programmes the 'Jubilee programmes'. In these three programmes, we see the kind of society that God had intended for Israel as they were being formed into a new nation after they were liberated from Egypt.

1. The Tithing Programme (Deut. 14)

At the end of every three years, bring all the tithes of that year's produce and store it in your towns, so that the Levites (who have no allotment or inheritance of their own) and the aliens, the fatherless and the widows who live in your towns may come and eat and be satisfied, and so that the LORD your God may bless you in all the work of your hands (Deut. 14:28).

When you have finished setting aside a tenth of all your produce in the third year, the year of the tithe, you shall give it to the Levite,

the alien, the fatherless and the widow, so that they may eat in
your towns and be satisfied (Deut. 26:12).

Picture the scene. Once every three years, the Israelites were to
leave their villages, taking with them a tenth (a tithe) of that
year's crops, herds and flocks. They were to travel to the nearest
town centre where they would deposit their tithe. The poor,
orphans, widows and foreigners (as well as the Levitical priests)
were then invited to come and help themselves to whatever they
needed.

Can we imagine a contemporary parallel? What would it be
like, for example, if every three years the big retailers such as
Walmart, Tesco, Marks & Spencer, McDonald's and so on were to
deposit one tenth of their goods in the town halls so that the poor
and marginalised could come and take what they needed? To our
modern-day, capitalist, consumerist minds, such an idea seems
extraordinary and radical. And yet it was what God instructed
his people to do on a regular basis – every three years. It was
intended to be an ordinary part of life in Israel, just like observing an annual festival. It was meant to be a demonstration of generosity and compassion by the people towards the poor.

2. The Sabbath Programme (Deut. 15; Lev. 25)

The three-yearly programme was an important mechanism in
itself for levelling out economic inequalities and encouraging a
spirit of generosity. But God did not stop there. Every seventh
year, the sabbath year, God required the nation to do three things:

i) Proclaim a year's holiday (Lev. 25)

That's right. A one-year holiday for everyone:

> 'For six years sow your fields, and for six years prune your vine-
> yards and gather their crops. But in the seventh year the land is to

have a sabbath of rest, a sabbath to the LORD. Do not sow your fields or prune your vineyards. Do not reap what grows of itself or harvest the grapes of your untended vines. The land is to have a year of rest' (Lev. 25:3–5).

The land was to be left uncultivated. There was to be no work but instead enforced rest for everyone, including the servants, hired workers, animals and the land, for a whole year.

The people and the land were linked in their shared need for rest from labour. For those of us who view it merely as a commodity, this may seem an oddly anthropomorphic view of land, but perhaps we have lost sight of its covenantal, sacramental nature. The ecological benefits of allowing the land to rest are well known. Just as people have renewed energy levels after resting, so the land has increased fertility after lying fallow for a period of time.

But if the people did not work for a year, how were they going to survive? God anticipated this concern: 'You may ask, "What will we eat in the seventh year if we do not plant or harvest our crops?"' God's reply was that he would:

'Send you such a blessing in the sixth year that the land will yield enough for three years. While you plant during the eighth year, you will eat from the old crop and will continue to eat from it until the harvest of the ninth year comes in' (Lev. 25:20–22).

In other words, the harvest from the first six years will be sufficient to feed the people for nine years. This was an amazing promise. Furthermore, food that grew naturally could also be eaten:

'Whatever the land yields during the sabbath year will be food for you – for yourself, your manservant and maidservant, and the hired worker and temporary resident who live among you, as well as for your livestock and the wild animals in your land. Whatever the land produces may be eaten' (Lev. 25:6,7).

Exodus includes an extra humanitarian point here:

'For six years you are to sow your fields and harvest the crops, but during the seventh year let the land lie unploughed and unused. Then the poor among your people may get food from it, and the wild animals may eat what they leave. Do the same with your vineyard and your olive grove' (Ex. 23:10,11).

The poor, then, were to benefit from the land being left fallow, for they were to be allowed to help themselves to the crops that grew during that period. This has echoes of the three-yearly pro-gramme on tithing.

God was teaching his people a number of things by means of this sabbath law:

- that they could and should trust him for their survival. They did not have to worry about what they would eat during this year of holiday. God would provide for their needs;
- that the land and its produce really belonged to him, not them. The people had no ownership rights over the food that grew during the seventh year. It was to be eaten by everyone, even the wild animals;
- that his people were not to exploit their fellow people. For ser-vants and hired workers, this was serious 'good news';
- that his people were not to exploit the land or the animals. The nation was to be responsible in its stewardship of God's cre-ation.

ii) Cancel all debts (Deut. 15)

'At the end of every seven years you must cancel debts. This is how it is to be done: Every creditor shall cancel the loan he has made to his fellow Israelite. He shall not require payment from his fellow Israelite or brother, because the LORD's time for cancelling debts has been proclaimed' (Deut. 15:1,2).

This was an incredible law. Once every seven years, there was a mechanism that evened out any gross inequalities between the haves and the have-nots, and prevented people descending into excessive poverty. This was tough for the wealthy lenders, of course, but as the Old Testament scholar E.W. Heaton has said, the law was not designed 'for good business but for good community'.[1] The principle is that debt should be limited and people should not be encumbered with debt in perpetuity.

And this was really the heart of the matter. God was making it clear through these programmes that he was far more concerned with healthy relationships than with material prosperity. He was also more concerned with the motives of people's hearts than with their adherence to the letter of the law. Consequently, he warned them against harbouring bad attitudes and violating the spirit of the law:

> 'Do not be hard-hearted or tight-fisted towards your poor brother. Rather be open-handed and freely lend him whatever he needs. Be careful not to harbour this wicked thought: "The seventh year, the year for cancelling debts, is near," so that you do not show ill will towards your needy brother and give him nothing. He may then appeal to the LORD against you, and you will be found guilty of sin' (Deut. 15:7–9).

iii) Release all slaves (Deut. 15)

The third thing that God required of the nation during the sabbath year was to release all slaves: 'If a fellow Hebrew, a man or woman, sells himself to you and serves you six years, in the

---

[1] E.W. Heaton, *The Hebrew Kingdoms*.

seventh year you must let him go free' (Deut. 15:12). The wealthy
of the day could afford slaves. It was a sign of their prosperity.
Now God was instructing them to release their slaves every
seven years. God was teaching his people about freedom. They
had been slaves once in Egypt but he had miraculously set them
free. Therefore, they were not to keep others in a state of permanent slavery.

Not only that, but they were to be magnanimous with their
leaving gifts: 'And when you release him, do not send him away
empty-handed. Supply him liberally from your flock, your thresh-
ing-floor and your winepress. Give to him as the LORD your God
has blessed you' (Deut. 15:13,14). They were to give generously,
just as they had themselves received generously from God.

Once again, however, God showed that he was more concerned with the spirit of the law than the letter of it. The purpose
of the law was to give the slaves their freedom, but if they exercised that freedom by choosing to stay with their master that was
fine, too (Deut. 15:16,17). They didn't have to go if they didn't
want to. Otherwise the law would have been counter-productive,
constraining rather than releasing.

In summary, as the sabbath year was enforced, debts and
slaves were released. The Septuagint (often abbreviated as LXX;
the Greek Old Testament) uses the word *aphesis* for 'release'. We
will encounter this word later in the New Testament when it is
translated as 'forgiveness' of sins or debts. The sabbath year
brought together not only sound ecological and humanitarian
principles. It also grounded the people in faith in a God who
always acts to give them sabbath rest.

God promised that if the nation obeyed his commands 'there
would be no poor among them' (Deut. 15:4–6). This was a thun-
derbolt statement. An outrageous promise! No modern day
politician would dare campaign on this agenda. But it is here as
a promise by God for obedience to the sabbath year. Sadly, this
promise was not fulfilled in the Old Testament. It was only

fulfilled 1,500 years later by the early church in Acts, but we are getting ahead of our story!

3. The Jubilee Programme (Lev. 25)

The third programme was the Jubilee programme. Here God required the nation to do four things every fifty years:

i) Proclaim one year's holiday

The word Jubilee comes from the Hebrew word *yobhel*, meaning 'ram's horn'. The sound of the ram's horn being blown on the Day of Atonement signalled the commencement of the Jubilee year and ushered in the year's holiday. This requirement was a repetition of the sabbath programme. We will see later (in chapter 4) how the concept of sabbath rest came to represent the whole of the Jubilee programmes and principles.

ii) Cancel debts

Debt cancellation was also a part of the sabbath year programme. There was a real appropriateness about debts being cancelled on the Day of Atonement. On this day, the high priest drew lots between two goats. One was sacrificed to atone for the nation's sins and the other was led into the wilderness to show that the sins of the nation were carried away. The day represented both a vertical reconciliation between God and man, and a horizontal reconciliation between man and his neighbour. The debts were wiped clean along both axes.

iii) Release slaves

The release of slaves, like a year's holiday and debt cancellation, was also a provision of the sabbath programme. This time, however, slaves had the right not only to be released but also to return to the property of their forefathers (Lev. 25:41), thanks to the next provision, unique to the year of Jubilee.

iv) Return all properties bought

In the year of Jubilee, God required everyone who had bought houses and fields to return all properties to their original owners:

> 'If one of your countrymen becomes poor and sells some of his property, his nearest relative is to come and redeem what his countryman has sold. If, however, a man has no-one to redeem it for him but he himself prospers and acquires sufficient means to redeem it, he is to determine the value for the years since he sold it and refund the balance to the man to whom he sold it; he can then go back to his own property. But if he does not acquire the means to repay him, what he sold will remain in the possession of the buyer until the Year of Jubilee. It will be returned in the Jubilee, and he can then go back to his property' (Lev. 25:25–28).

The three previous requirements had been tough enough, but this truly was an outrageous demand. But let us see God's reasoning behind this demand. As we shall see in the next chapter, when the nation of Israel entered the Promised Land, the country was divided up in an equitable manner. The territories were divided up in proportion to the size of the tribes. Once each tribe had their allocation, the land was further divided up according to clans and families, again according to size but this time the area was chosen by drawing lots. Each family began life in the Promised Land as landowners of their own plots. In a primarily agricultural economy, this land was the means whereby each family sustained itself.

However, when families fell into hardship through misfortune, accidents or over-consumption they got into debt. If the debt could not be repaid, the land had to be sold and the families moved off the land. Once the land was sold, family members migrated into towns looking for work – usually as servants or day labourers. This pattern can still be seen in many parts of the developing world today. The traditional support of the extended family disintegrated with this process of migration and urbanisation. The safety net of the family and clan did not exist for these migrant workers once they left home.

Nations that experience this kind of trend invariably develop societies with economic inequalities. Imagine, then, a society where every fifty years all properties are returned to their original owners. At the sound of the ram's horn on the Day of Atonement, the migrant labourers and slaves were released and returned to their village and their original plot of land. When they returned, they were reunited with members of their extended family. Family relationships were restored. They were able to sit under their vines and fig trees again in peace, sharing meals and conversation.

The return of properties to their original owners every fifty years had important implications for the sale of land:

> 'If you sell land to one of your countrymen or buy any from him, do not take advantage of each other. You are to buy from your countryman on the basis of the number of years since the Jubilee. And he is to sell to you on the basis of the number of years left for harvesting crops. When the years are many, you are to increase the price, and when the years are few, you are to decrease the price, because what he is really selling you is the number of crops. Do not take advantage of each other, but fear your God' (Lev. 25:14–17).

In practice, the people were not really selling their land but rather leasing it out for a fifty-year period. God was therefore also reminding his people through this Jubilee mechanism that he alone was the true owner of the land.

As much as Jubilee was about the even distribution of wealth and assets, it was also about the rediscovery of family life. The distribution of wealth was a means of equalising society so that every fifty years each family had an opportunity to start afresh – free of debt and in possession of their own land. This prevented a situation whereby economic inequalities grew wider and wider only to be equilibrated through violent revolution. But the return of properties also meant that family relationships could be restored. The Jubilee programme was therefore deeply pro-community, deeply pro-relationship.

To really understand the impact of these three programmes, we need to look at the fifty-year grid below, where (a) represents the tithing programme (every three years), (b) the sabbath programme (every seven years) and (c) the Jubilee programme (every fifty years). In a fifty-year cycle, the tithing programme would occur sixteen times, the sabbath programme seven times and the Jubilee programme once. This was a devastating, challenging set of demands!

1	11	21a+b	31	41
2	12a	22	32	42a+b
3a	13	23	33a	43
4	14b	24a	34	44
5	15a	25	35b	45a
6a	16	26	36a	46
7b	17	27a	37	47
8	18a	28b	38	48a
9a	19	29	39a	49b
10	20	30a	40	50c

a 3-yr
b 7-yr
c 50-yr

Years 6/7, 14/15, 27/28 and 35/36 were particularly demand-ing years for wealthy Israelites. In each case, a tithing year was immediately followed by a sabbath year. After they had already given away 10 per cent of their assets in the previous year, they had to announce a year's holiday for everyone the following year, release all their slaves and cancel all the debts owed to them. This was going to be a real test of their faith. But God promised his people that he would richly bless them if they only trusted and obeyed (Deut. 15:4,5; Lev. 26).

The full impact of the programmes, however, came at the end of the fifty-year cycle. Year 48 was a tithing year, year 49 a sab-bath year and year 50 was a Jubilee year. A triple whammy! The demands were great in terms of obedience and generosity, but the Israelites would have realised that God was also giving them two consecutive years holiday. In other words, two consecutive years where the nation could not grow their crops and farm their land. Good news for the slaves, animals and land, but the people had a right to ask what they were going to eat if they could neither plant nor harvest their crops. God assured them that there would be sufficient left over from their previous harvest to last them until when they could plant and harvest their crops again.

This was a truly amazing vision for a just society. What politician today would have the courage to campaign for election with this manifesto? In the absence of a state-run welfare system, the respon-sibility for the poor and marginalised rested with each member of the nation through their practice of Jubilee *shalom* (the Jewish concept of *shalom* was more than simply inner peace. It was about whole-someness in relation to God, neighbour and creation). This was a bot-tom up, rather than our modern top down, system of welfare.

Jubilee Principles

What principles lay at the heart of the Jubilee programmes? What values was God seeking to promote through their observance?

We have already touched on a number of them, but it is worth restating them in full:

Social holiness

The Jubilee programmes were God's mechanism for restoring the socio-economic order he had intended, by means of a regular redistribution of wealth and assets. God was seeking to create a society that was holistic in its approach to holiness, a society that reflected his nature and character by caring for the poor, the oppressed, the defenceless and the disadvantaged, and giving them sabbath rest. The reason for wanting a society expressing social holiness is so that he can fulfil his grand objective: 'I will put my dwelling place among you, and I will not abhor you. I will walk among you and be your God' (Lev. 26:11,12). This desire of God's to live and walk with his people goes right back to Adam in Genesis and it has not changed. He still wants to dwell with his people, but because he is holy, his people also have to be holy. The idea of God dwelling ('tabernacling') and walking among his people is a consistent theme in Exodus (Ex. 25:8) through to Jesus (Jn.1:14) and Revelation (Rev. 21:3). This is God's desire and therefore his people have to be holy in every aspect of their lives, including their economics.

Faith

The Jubilee programmes demanded a practical exercising of faith. Despite God's assurances that he would bless their obedience, it was going to be tough for the Israelites, particularly those who had the potential to become rich at the expense of others. In a fallen world, their natural inclinations would have been much like our own: to accumulate as much wealth as possible and to do so in competition with their neighbours. However, God was their King and he wanted the nation to trust him for everything – from economic provision to his unique ways of fighting battles.

Liberty

The Jubilee programmes were about liberty – economic, emotional and spiritual freedom. The good news is about setting captives free and remission of debts. This freedom was not just for the poor, the debtors, the slaves; it was also for the wealthy who were at risk of being ensnared by greed. God wanted all of his people to experience the freedom of dependency on him.

Stewardship

The Jubilee programmes taught the nation about stewardship – of the land and each other. God was the ultimate owner of everyone and everything, but they had a duty of care towards his creation. The poor and disadvantaged were the responsibility of everyone, especially the wealthy. The Israelites' stewardship of the land was to be in the form of private ownership, not on a freehold basis, but on a fifty-year leasehold. This was meant to prevent greed (adding house to house and joining field to field – cf. Is. 5:8) and excessive land valuation. It also encouraged an appreciation of the ephemeral nature of life. Similarly, Israelite slaves could not be permanently owned, and were consequently only to be tied into a seven-year contract.

Family

The Jubilee programmes were about the rediscovery of family life and the restoration of relationships. The return of properties every fifty years to their original owners was an important mechanism for maintaining the family/clan/kinship structure that God had instituted. Furthermore, the regular cancellation of debts meant that those with surplus resources were discouraged from lending outside their own clan.

Generosity

The key characteristic of Jubilee was generosity – extraordinary generosity. This generosity was not the charity variety where the rich live in one place or country and the poor another. The generous acts of the Jubilee programmes ensured that the poor were provided for and belonged to their community. There is no word either in Hebrew or Greek for 'generosity'. Instead the Hebrew words used are *chesed* (mercy, loving kindness) and *rachamim* (compassion, pity, to love) and the Greek words are *eleos* (mercy, loving kindness) and *oiktirmon* (merciful, compassionate). Generosity is therefore the same as mercy. Everywhere Jubilee is practised, we will see extravagant generosity through acts of mercy. The word for 'alms or charity' (Mt. 6:1–4) is *eleemosyne* and is probably better translated as 'acts of mercy or generosity'.

In a sense, the Jubilee programmes are the practical outworking of God's command to 'love the LORD your God with all your heart and with all your soul and with all your strength' (Deut. 6:5) and to 'love your neighbour as yourself' (Lev. 19:18). If we love God in this way, we will trust him to provide for our needs and love justice as he does. If we love our neighbour as ourselves, expressions of generosity through debt cancellation, the tithe and giving *shabbat* (rest) make sense. God's express purpose in taking the people out of Egypt was to make them into 'a kingdom of priests and a holy nation' (Ex. 19:6). This is what a holy nation looks like.

The Jubilee programmes give us a vision of *shalom* – a society at peace with itself and experiencing God's blessing. It is impossible to study them without feeling challenged, without wondering what a modern-day application of their principles might look like. God clearly prefers a just society to mere Christian philanthropy. What are the implications for us today?

This is a big and challenging question, and one which we will attempt to answer. To do it justice, however, we first need to see what else the Bible has to say about the Jubilee programmes – their context, their purpose and their outworking in both the Old and New Testaments.

3

Chosen People, Promised Land

To fully appreciate the significance and impact of the Jubilee programmes we need to understand something of their background.
As we've said before, the subject of the Jubilee raises the questions: 'What kind of people are we supposed to be? How does
God want his people to live?' The Jubilee programmes were originally given to a group of ex-slaves wandering in the wilderness
of Sinai en route to a better life in the Promised Land. They were
introduced as a part of the overall objective to form a new nation
that would reflect God's character.

To move from slavery to nationhood required some significant
changes on the part of the people. A number of features about
this nation of former slaves are worth highlighting. First, God's
strategy of redemption did not focus on redeeming isolated individuals. It centred on the formation of a new nation, a new social
order where the community of people would live in the way
intended by their Creator. When God called Moses to lead the
Israelites out of Egypt, he promised, 'I will take you as my own
people' (Ex. 6:7). Not as individuals, but as a people.

Second, their relationships with God and one another would
be different. In their worship, there would be no more human
sacrifices, sexual orgies or idols. They would worship God in a
simple collapsible tent called a tabernacle, not in a sophisticated
temple. This was all very different from the surrounding nations.
And in their human relationships, the Israelites were to show

respect to parents, the elderly, the opposite sex, neighbours, slaves, foreigners and for each other's property.

Third, there was an innovative new way to manage healthcare. A quarantine system was introduced for the first time to tackle communicable diseases. There were instructions on managing the sewage system, hand washing, food preparation and storage.

Fourth, God gave them laws to ensure their community was based on justice. The judiciary system must be fair. The economic arrangements must enable each family to make a dignified living. There must be special provisions for the poor, widows and orphans – those who lose their place in the community through poverty or death of a husband or father. Furthermore there were laws on lending, land ownership, interest rates and harvesting designed to ensure a just humanitarian society where social holiness would be evident. We have already mentioned that in Hebrew thinking, there is no secular-sacred divide. For the Jews, faith is all-embracing touching every area of life right down to loans, interest rates and how you harvest your fields.

God gave the nation new laws in order to reflect his holiness: 'Be holy as I am holy' (Lev. 11:44,45; see also 1 Pet. 1:15,16). The phrase 'before the Lord' is used sixty times in Leviticus and simply means 'set apart or consecrate' (Hebrew: *kadosh*). They were told that everything in their daily lives had to be carried out as 'before the Lord'. In other words, God saw everything that they did – at home, at work and in the tabernacle – and therefore everything was to be holy before God. Not just personal holiness but a corporate social holiness that would set them apart from the way other nations lived, a 'kingdom of priests and a holy nation' (Ex. 19:6). They were to be different in every aspect of their lives.

The Israelites' years in the wilderness were not easy. They were sometimes short of food, meat in particular, and it did not take long before camping lost its appeal: 'If only we had died by the LORD's hand in Egypt! There we sat round pots of meat and ate all the food we wanted, but you have brought us out into this desert to starve this entire assembly to death' (Ex. 16:3).

And yet God provided for all their needs: 'These forty years the LORD your God has been with you, and you have not lacked anything' (Deut. 2:7). And poetically God said that 'their shoes did not wear out'. The wilderness experience was a time for the nation to learn dependence on God and trust him to provide for all their needs.

After forty years of wandering in the Sinai wilderness (Deut. 8:2–5), where they were humbled and tested, God at last brought them to the land he had promised. They would change from a nomadic community to a settled one, and the transition would prove challenging. A settled community with fixed assets – land, farms and property – was perhaps even less likely to embrace an attitude of dependence on God. He therefore warned them about falling prey to pride and greed: 'You may say to yourself, "My power and the strength of my hands have produced this wealth for me." But remember the LORD your God, for it is he who gives you the ability to produce wealth, and so confirms his covenant, which he swore to your forefathers, as it is today' (Deut. 8:17,18).

As they transitioned into a settled community, God gave them instructions on the structure of civil society, how the land was to be divided up among the twelve tribes and the laws that govern community life. We will look at each of these aspects in turn.

The Kinship Structure of Israel

The society in Israel was based on kinship. Israel was one large family of blood brothers sharing a common ancestor and history. The largest unit was the *tribe* (Hebrew: *shevet*) of which there were twelve. When Levi was set aside as a tribe dedicated to serve in the worship of the tabernacle and temple, the tribe of Joseph, being the largest, was split in two – Ephraim and Manasseh – so that the twelve tribes could be retained. The size of the tribes varied from a few thousand in the case of Dan (during the period of the Judges) to perhaps 100,000 in the case of Judah (during the monarchy).

The second largest unit was the *clan* (Hebrew: *mishpahah*). In seven of the tribes, the clans were named after Jacob's grandsons; in the other five tribes, the clans were named after his great-grandsons. There were approximately sixty clans. The total adult male population of Israel at the time of entering Canaan was 600,000 as given in Numbers 26:51. The average size of a clan was around 10,000 adult males. The clan had common interests and duties, and their members were conscious of the blood-bond that united them; they called each other 'brothers' (1 Sam. 20:29).

The smallest family unit recognised in the Hebrew language was what sociologists and theologians call the '*3G-family*' (Hebrew: *bethav*). This was a three- to four-generation family living in neighbouring houses on the same plot of land. It would also include non-kinship members, as adoption seems to have been a common practice as a means of absorbing the poor, needy and foreigners into the kinship system of Israel. Critically, there was no word for the nuclear family in Israelite vocabulary. Instead there were extended family units of 10–30 adults. The scholar Gottwald believes that the 3G-family may have contained as many as 50–100 persons. Whenever the Bible speaks about family, it includes what we now call the extended family as well as God's larger family. This was the bottom rung of social institutions in Israelite society.

Each person, then, was anchored within a series of concentric circles of belonging. Each was a member of a small group (extended family), within a bigger group (clan), within a still bigger group (tribe) and within a whole (Israel). It was a structure that united people, giving them a common identity and purpose whilst also providing various layers of protection and accountability.

The Division of the Land

The original division of the land was based on the size of the tribes. Reuben, Gad and half the tribe of Manasseh were allocated land east of the Jordan, at their request. They were the first to claim their land, but Joshua urged them to help the other tribes lay hold of their inheritance on the other side of the Jordan (Joshua 1:12–15). They agreed to do so. Leaving their wives, children and livestock behind, the men crossed the Jordan with the other tribes and fought alongside them. Judah, Ephraim and the other half of the tribe of Manasseh took land west of the river. The remaining seven tribes were slow to claim their inheritance, but Joshua instructed them to divide up the rest of the land and make a survey of it. Once they had done this, he distributed the land amongst them 'according to their tribal divisions' (Josh. 18:10).

Six cities, three on either side of the Jordan, were then set apart as 'cities of refuge'. These were cities where anyone who accidentally killed a person could flee and find asylum from the 'avenger of blood' (Josh. 20).

That left the Levites, who still needed towns to live in and pasture-lands for their livestock. They had not been given a territorial inheritance, unlike the other tribes, because they had been set apart for priestly duties. The Lord himself was their inheritance (Josh. 13:33). But they needed a place to live and some land for their animals. Each of the tribes therefore gave the Levites a number of towns and pasture-lands from their own inheritance (see map in Appendix).

Straightaway we have some hints of what kind of society God was seeking to establish. It was to be a society based on the principles of *solidarity* (Joshua exhorting Reuben, Gad and the half-tribe of Manasseh fighting for their brothers: 'You are to help your brothers until the LORD gives them rest, as he has done for you' (Josh. 1:14,15)), *fairness* (the land was divided according to the size of the tribes: 'To a larger group give a larger inheritance, and to a smaller group a smaller one' (Num. 33:54)), *mercy* (the provision of cities of refuge – in order to spare the accused of murder from blood vengeance if it could be proved that the cause of death was accidental) and *generosity* (the giving of towns to the Levites and their renunciation of a material inheritance encouraged an attitude of sacrificial giving – to both God and man). Underpinning all of these principles was an attitude of *trust*, that God would honour their obedience and provide for all their needs.

The land was therefore divided up on a tribal basis, but the day-to-day management of the land and of social relationships fell to the clans and extended families. These two groups had boundaries that blurred and overlapped. The clan was responsible for the protection of people and preservation of property. This responsibility was personalised and fell to the clan member who was most closely related to the person in need. This would usually be a family member. The role was referred to as that of the '*goel*' (redeemer, from '*gaal*' – to redeem). If no close family member was found to fulfil the role then it fell to a clansman (Lev. 25:49).

There were several facets to the role of redeemer. The first was to preserve the property and name of a fellow clansman. Thus the '*goel*' had to:

a) raise up an heir if the kinsman died without children (Deut. 25:5);
b) buy back an individual who had sold himself into slavery or indentured service through debt or need (Lev. 25:49);
c) buy back property sold by a member of the clan because of debt or need (Lev. 25:25);
d) inherit the land and thus keep it within the family or at least the clan (Num. 27:11).

These aspects of the kinsman's (*goel's*) role can be seen in the story of Ruth and Boaz. Boaz was a member of the same clan as

Elimelech (Ruth 2:1). He was therefore a kinsman, but since he was not the nearest relative he did not immediately fulfil the role of the *'goel'* (Ruth 2:20). This responsibility had to be declined by others before it came to him and he was able to marry Ruth (Ruth 3:12). Boaz then fulfilled the role of *'goel'*, raising up an heir for Elimelech and also inheriting the family land: 'I have also acquired Ruth the Moabitess, Mahlon's widow, as my wife, in order to maintain the name of the dead with his property, so that his name will not disappear from among his family or from the town records' (Ruth 4:10).

The name and the land thus remained linked and the relationship between the two was preserved.

It is interesting to note that the responsibilities of the *goel* were carried out even though Ruth was a foreigner. Indeed, Boaz was praised for his actions (Ruth 4:14). His kindness bore good fruit: a son was born to them, Obed, whose grandson was King David, from whom can be traced the human lineage of Jesus.

As well as carrying responsibility for the protection of property, the *goel* had a further role of personal protection. In the case of murder, the *goel* became the *'goel haddam'*, the redeemer – or avenger – of blood. It was then his responsibility to pursue the murderers of a kinsman and bring them to justice (Deut. 19:12). It is interesting that the figure of the *goel* reflects that of God in his relationship with Israel grounded in the covenant. He too is a kinsman redeemer and he calls his people to act in the same manner.

The family and clan were therefore God's chosen structures for ensuring that the weak and the needy would be cared for in Israel. They were designed by him to be institutions of grace, extending love and mercy to the poor, the widows, the fatherless, the foreigner (Deut. 15:7, 10:18). They were his unequivocal response to Cain's unanswered question in Genesis 4:9 – 'Am I my brother's keeper?'

The People and the Land

What, then, was the nature of the Israelites' relationship with the land they now inhabited, the Promised Land? Right back in Genesis 12:1 we read that when God first called Abram, he said to him: 'Leave your country, your people and your father's household and go to the land I will show you.' Later, when Abram reaches Canaan, God makes a covenant with him and declares: 'To your descendants I give this land, from the river of Egypt to the great river, the Euphrates' (Gen. 15:18). The land was therefore an integral part of God's covenantal relationship with his people. It is striking in this regard to note that the word Israel came to denote both the people (originally one person – Jacob) and their land. The two became inextricably bound up together.

If we examine the basis of the land-holding system in ancient Israel, we uncover some interesting parallels between God's relationship towards his people and his relationship towards the land. The bottom line in both cases was that they ultimately belonged to God – 'The earth is the LORD's, and everything in it, the world, and all who live in it' (Ps. 24:1). The fact of God's ownership placed serious limitations on how both the people and the land were to be treated. Since the people of Israel belonged to God, they were not to be subject to any foreign authority – hence God told Pharaoh to let his people go and intervened miraculously to liberate them (Ex. 7–14). Nor, however, were they to be subject to one another in any binding or absolute way. Rather, they were to have an attitude of stewardship towards each other. We have already seen some of the implications of this type of relationship when considering the role of the kinsman redeemer. The implications for the land were similar. It was given to the Israelites on trust, but was not ultimately theirs to do whatever they liked with: 'The land is mine' declares God in Leviticus 25:23. Richard Foster puts it succinctly, 'In the Bible, God's absolute rights as owner and our relative rights as stewards are unmistakably clear.'[1]

Two important points flow from this fact of God's rights as owner. Firstly, the land, like the people, could not be permanently sold. Since God was the real owner, the family who possessed the land only really had it on lease. As leaseholders, they did not have the authority to sell it on permanently. Every clan and each extended family within it possessed their land in perpetuity. To provide some necessary flexibility, they could lease it out to another, but only until the next Jubilee Year. This allowed those in grave financial distress some way out of their difficulties but without permitting outright sale. There was no freehold market for land in Israel.

We know from history that it is the distress sale of land that has made it possible for some to accumulate huge landholdings while others have been made permanently landless. If many families lost control of their land through leasing it out and moving away, a massive social movement would become necessary for them to re-establish ownership of their ancestral land. Such a massive periodic upheaval was exactly what was envisaged in Lev. 25:28. We will look at this in more detail in the next chapter.

Secondly, the land was distributed equally in order that wealth and power would not become concentrated in the hands of a few but would rather be shared. At the time, Israel was an agricultural economy, hence people derived their livelihood from the land. They needed land to build a home, but they also needed it to produce food and thereby sustain themselves. By giving each family a landholding roughly equivalent in size to their neighbour's, each was given a fair opportunity to earn a dignified living. Although in practice the quality of the land varied from family to family – in terms of type of soil, access to water etc. (cf. Josh. 15:19) – there was nonetheless an essential fairness in the distribution.

---

[1] Richard Foster, *Money, Sex and Power*.

And no one was to take it upon himself to re-divide the land.
Moving boundary stones (to encroach upon the territory of anoth-
er) would incur God's wrath and vengeance (see Deut. 19:14;
Prov. 23:10; Hos. 5:10).

Israel's tightly controlled system of land ownership had a
number of ramifications:

- *Size of towns*
  The strong emphasis on family ownership of the land discouraged mass migration to the cities. Therefore Israel experienced
  no significant large-scale urbanisation. The typical pattern of
  urbanisation that we see today was prevented by the way
  Israel protected the poor from becoming permanently landless
  and being driven off the land. The pattern in Israel was 'free
  peasants on small land holdings of equal size'.[2]
- *Class system*
  The limitations placed on land acquisition in Israel restricted
  the development of a class-based social structure. In any society, land, and the property built on it, is the major form in
  which wealth is held. Israel was unique among societies in the
  ancient world in its denunciation of class distinctions and the
  centralised state.
- *Social welfare*
  The land ownership system had its roots within the kinship
  structure of Israel. Shared familial ownership of the land
  implied shared responsibility towards the members of the family and clan. The care of the disadvantaged and marginalised
  was thus institutionalised. It was not left to the State but was
  the responsibility of everyone – the individual, the extended
  family, the clan and the tribe. As Walter Brueggemann has said,
  the Old Testament takes neither a capitalist nor a communist
  approach to social welfare: 'It rather urges a quite alternative

---

[2] Roland de Vaux, *Ancient Israel: Its Life and Institutions*.

reading of human community that can only be described as covenantal. Property must be managed, valued and distributed so that every person of the community is honoured and so that the well-being of each is intimately tied to that of the others.'[3]

Unfortunately, we do not have to read far into the Old Testament before we discover that the Israelites struggled to remain faithful to God and eventually decided that they wanted a king to rule over them like the nations that surrounded them. God warned his people of the injustices that would occur under such leadership (1 Sam. 8:6–20), but they would not be deterred. The way of life that the Israelites knew during the period of the Judges was to collapse. Nonetheless, the original forms of social welfare remained God's best plan for his people. Indeed, equitable land ownership and personal security recurs as a part of the vision for the future new kingdom: 'but they shall all sit under their own vines and under their own fig trees, and no one shall make them afraid; for the mouth of the LORD of hosts has spoken' (Mich. 4:4, NRSV).

Laws Governing Community Life

We have looked at the interplay between God, his people and the land, and we have considered some of the laws God instituted for this new nation. Let us now take a more comprehensive look at the purpose and scope of the laws God gave to his people.

Israel was to be quite unlike the other nations surrounding her. The Israelites were to reflect God's holy character. Holiness was never going to come naturally to a people born into a fallen world, so God gave the Israelites laws to live by. These laws governed every aspect of community life: from personal hygiene to sexual purity, from the care of animals to the protection of

---

[3] Walter Brueggemann, *A Social Reading of the Old Testament*.

property, from the carrying out of sacrifices to the treatment of foreigners, from the celebration of festivals to the raising of children. God's purpose was to create a society at peace with him and at peace with itself, a society embracing *shalom*.

It is not within the scope of this book to look at all the laws God instituted for his people, but let us consider some of them as they relate to the subject in hand.

Lending

The classic way in which a peasant family disintegrated, due to debt, was as follows:

- Debt was incurred – either out of need or more often through over-consumption.
- Following a bad harvest or some natural catastrophe, the land was sold to pay off the debt.
- The members of the extended family, now landless, migrated to the city in search of work and became physically separated from the clan and extended family. They lost the support of the kinship and community.

God did not prohibit lending, but he carefully circumscribed the rights of the lender in order to protect the debtor from exploitation. Furthermore, the attempt to restrain lending in Israel was an important mechanism to protect the extended family from getting caught in a downward spiral of debt. It was rooted in a concern for the poor. We have already seen in the previous chapter that debts were to be cancelled every seven years. This was perhaps God's most challenging requirement with regards to lending, but there were a couple of other extremely important stipulations. Firstly, interest could not be charged:

> If you lend money to one of my people among you who is needy, do not be like a money-lender; charge him no interest (Ex. 22:25).

'If one of your countrymen becomes poor and is unable to support himself among you, help him as you would an alien or a temporary resident, so that he can continue to live among you. Do not take interest of any kind from him, but fear your God . . . You must not lend him money at interest or sell him food at a profit' (Lev. 25:35–37).

Do not charge your brother interest, whether on money or food or anything else that may earn interest (Deut. 23:19).

This is an extraordinary law. Many of us today live in nations that have founded their economic success on the principle of loans and interest. Consider the average house-buyer in the United Kingdom, for example, weighed down by a hefty mortgage for a period of twenty years or more. Even forgetting all the other provisions we have dealt with, if we merely put this law of zero-interest alongside the requirement to cancel debts every seven years, we cannot help but realise how far our own societies have strayed from God's vision of economic justice and wealth distribution.

Secondly, although the lender could take an item as a pledge, he was not to show contempt for his brother's needs in so doing:

If you take your neighbour's cloak as a pledge, return it to him by sunset, because his cloak is the only covering he has for his body. What else will he sleep in? When he cries out to me, I will hear, for I am compassionate (Ex. 22:26,27).

Do not take a pair of millstones – not even the upper one – as security for a debt, because that would be taking a man's livelihood as security (Deut. 24:6).

When you make a loan of any kind to your neighbour, do not go into his house to get what he is offering as a pledge. Stay outside and let the man to whom you are making the loan bring the pledge out to you (Deut. 24:10,11).

Commenting on these last two injunctions in Deuteronomy, the Old Testament scholar E.W. Heaton remarks on God's sensitive concern for the poor. The lender, he notes, is forbidden 'to take as a pledge anything essential to life'. Not only that but God upholds the debtor's dignity and protects him from humiliation and aggression 'by forbidding the lender to march into the house of the debtor as though he owned the place. He must wait at the door.'[4]

Restitution and restoration

Exodus 22 and Deuteronomy 22 list various laws governing how restitution was to be made when goods were stolen or damaged, and how lost items were to be restored to their owner:

> If a man grazes his livestock in a field or vineyard and lets them stray and they graze in another man's field, he must make restitution from the best of his own field or vineyard (Ex. 22:5).

> If you see your brother's ox or sheep straying, do not ignore it but be sure to take it back to him . . . Do the same if you find your brother's donkey or his cloak or anything he loses. Do not ignore it (Deut. 22:1,3).

God was emphasising the personal responsibility of individuals not only to care for their own property but also to have respect for their neighbours' property. They were to value and promote their neighbours' welfare as much as their own.

---

[4] E.W. Heaton, *The Hebrew Kingdoms*.

Tithes and offerings

We have already come across the concept of tithing in our previous chapter about the Jubilee programmes. We saw that every three years the Israelites were to set aside a tenth of that year's produce and bring it to the town centres so that it could be distributed to those in need. However, this did not mean that the Israelites were exempt from tithing for two years out of every three. On the contrary, tithing was an ongoing obligation – during the other two years the tithe was just used differently.

On those years, the people were to take their tithes to the tabernacle, and then enjoy a communal meal together. It was a time of great celebration and rejoicing. Worship and feasting were commingled:

> Be sure to set aside a tenth of all that your fields produce each year. Eat the tithe of your grain, new wine and oil, and the firstborn of your herds and flocks in the presence of the LORD your God at the place he will choose as a dwelling for his Name, so that you may learn to revere the LORD your God always (Deut. 14:22,23).

Their tithe therefore provided the food for the communal meal. What was left of the tithe was then given to the Levites, priests and the poor. This was to be the usual procedure. Tithing was an expression of thanks to God for his generosity (cf. Gen. 28:20–22), yet a clearly intended outcome of tithing, as it is established in the Law, is that the Levites and priests could be supported and the poor provided with food. Tithing was another way that God showed his concern for the poor and destitute as well as providing for Levites and priests who were not given any land. Contrast this then to many modern uses of 'the tithe' which often go towards (under)funding full-time church workers (and so not caring for them in the same spirit shown to the Levites) and financing church building programmes and other aspects of 'infrastructure'. Yet how much of this is *directly* of benefit to the poor in the way the Old Testament law conceived it being? How much of our modern 'tithing' puts actual food in people's bellies (or offers some other dynamic equivalent)? We will return to the subject later on where the inadequacies of tithing is discussed in the New Testament.

As well as tithing, the Israelites were expected to make freewill offerings to the Lord. There was no fixed amount for these offerings but they were to be given over and above the tithe, as an expression of the Israelites' devotion to God.

Sacrifices

In addition to the ritual sacrifices that formed part of their festival celebrations (see below), the Israelites were required to make regular personal sacrifices to God. The nature of these sacrifices varied according to their context and purpose. Chapters 1 to 7 in Leviticus list a wide variety: burnt offerings, grain offerings, sin offerings, guilt offerings and fellowship offerings.

The religious significance of the sacrifices is clear: God was thanked and honoured for his mercy (in forgiving sins) and for his provision (in supplying their needs), but they also had an important humanitarian dimension. Once the offerings had been made, they were eaten by the priests or the people (with the exception of the burnt offering which was completely burnt). In particular, the poor benefited from these shared meals. The obligation to make regular offerings therefore had an important function not only in encouraging an attitude of humility before God but also in encouraging generosity towards one's neighbour.

Festivals

We have mentioned the fact that the Israelites observed a number of festivals, and that these had a sacrificial aspect. The following were celebrated annually:

- Passover and the Feast of Unleavened Bread (Lev. 23:4–8);
- Feast of Firstfruits (Lev. 23:9–14);
- Feast of Weeks (Pentecost) (Lev. 23:15–22);
- Feast of Trumpets (New Year's Day) (Lev. 23:23–25);
- Day of Atonement (Lev. 23:26–32);
- Feast of Tabernacles and the Last Great Day (Lev. 23:33–43).

Although these festivals were primarily an occasion for the people to come together to worship God, give thanks to him for his mercy and goodness and make offerings to him, they were also important occasions for honouring the poor. Every time there was a festival or feast there would be food. This food was for sharing with everyone, including the poor. This was their source of meat and cakes.

One significant feature of the life of Israel is the amount of time they spent 'eating and drinking', having meals with one another. Life seemed to be centred around meals and festivals. 'Eating bread' was important not only to meet physical needs, but it was a time for social interaction. This was a time for conversation, laughter and fellowship as well as an expression of belonging and solidarity with all fellow Israelites.

There was also a special injunction in the regulations for celebrating Pentecost that made provision for the poor: 'When you reap the harvest of your land, do not reap to the very edges of your field or gather the gleanings of your harvest. Leave them for the poor and alien. I am the LORD your God' (Lev. 23:22).

As well as the annual festivals that punctuated the year at regular intervals, the Israelites were also to celebrate the first day of each month (Num. 28:11–15), the day of the new moon. It was another occasion to gather together and share food. A number of the annual festivals actually coincided with this day.

Then of course there was the sabbath or '*shabbat*': 'For six days, work is to be done, but the seventh day shall be your holy day, a Sabbath of rest to the LORD' (Ex. 35:2). This was a weekly day of rest for all, including servants and even animals. It was a day of thankful remembrance that the people were free to have a sab-bath. Once they had been slaves in Egypt and now God had delivered them (Deut. 5:12–15). On this day, too, the people shared a meal together as a family.

When thinking about the Old Testament Law a common pic-ture both Christians and non-Christians alike can sometimes have is of Moses dramatically descending Mount Sinai – hair, beard and desert clothes all blowing in the wind – carrying two weighty, rough-hewn stone tablets with the Ten Commandments inscribed upon them. Somehow this image of a shortlist seems to sum up the Law for people. Yet the Law of Moses is the *Torah*, which means 'teachings', and refers to the first five books of the Bible (*Pentateuch*) as well as the Mosaic legislation. As such it cov-ers all the laws mentioned in the *Torah* not just the Ten Commandments and laws on relationships. The Law of Moses included the Jubilee programmes, laws on lending, interest rates, protection of property, social responsibility, farming and much more. Therefore if you didn't grant a sabbath year or a *shabbat* day of rest for employees, if you refused to cancel debts, instead charging interest on loans and defrauding the wages of employ-ees, these were as much about breaking the Law of Moses as were committing adultery or murder. The Law of Moses given by God was truly comprehensive and holistic. There was no secular-sacred divide: the whole of life was covered.

Thanks then to the weekly *shabbat* meals, the multitude of fes-tivals and sacrifices and the laws on gleaning, it was intended that the poor should never go hungry. When we add to these the kinship structure of Israel, the laws governing land ownership, interest and property and most importantly the Jubilee pro-grammes, we start to appreciate what an extraordinary kind of society God was seeking to establish – just and merciful and rooted in humility (cf. Mich. 6:8). With such a comprehensive array of protective mechanisms, no one should ever have fallen into serious need or below a certain level of poverty. Gross economic disparities should never have occurred amongst the people. But they did, and we shall see how and why they did in the next chapter.

4

Jubilee in the Old Testament

Sadly, there is no evidence that the Jubilee programmes were ever observed in any regular or cyclical way once the Israelites had occupied the Promised Land. The reason for this is largely because of humankind's self-centeredness. There were no personal benefits for showing generosity to others, especially the marginalised and vulnerable. Despite their humbling and testing in the wilderness, trusting God to provide for their needs was a lesson they had not learnt. It was easier to trust in their own abilities to provide for themselves. Solidarity, justice and compassion were difficult for the new settlers of the land. The Jubilee laws were costly in financial terms. Just because God had provided his people with a comprehensive set of laws governing community life, it did not automatically mean that they needed to obey them . . . All this despite God's instructions to Joshua as he led the people across the Jordan river into Canaan: 'Be careful to obey all the law my servant Moses gave you . . . Do not let this Book of the Law depart from your mouth' (Josh. 1:7,8).

Blessings for Obedience, Punishments for Disobedience

When the laws were given to the Israelites, God made plain to them what the consequences would be of both obedience and disobedience. If they obeyed, he promised them blessings:

'I will send you rain in its season, and the ground will yield its crops and the trees of the field their fruit. Your threshing will continue until grape harvest and the grape harvest will continue until planting, and you will eat all the food you want and live in safety in your land. I will grant peace in the land, and you will lie down and no-one will make you afraid. I will remove savage beasts from the land, and the sword will not pass through your country . . . I will look on you with favour and make you fruitful and increase your numbers, and I will keep my covenant with you. You will still be eating last year's harvest when you will have to move it out to make room for the new. I will put my dwelling-place among you, and I will not abhor you. I will walk among you and be your God, and you will be my people' (Lev. 26:4–12).

The fruitfulness of the land and the assurance of material provision and security were central to God's promises. He was setting forth a vision of social harmony that harked back to Eden – the land yielding its food without painful toil, no violence between man and his neighbour, no threat from savage animals, and God walking amongst his people. The punishments for disobedience, on the other hand, contained echoes of Adam's punishment in the Garden of Eden. Once again, the breakdown of relationship with God would lead to a breakdown of people's relationship with the natural world and with their neighbours. Furthermore, just as Adam was expelled from the Garden of Eden, so the Israelites would be expelled from their land:

'I will . . . make the sky above you like iron and the ground beneath you like bronze. Your strength will be spent in vain, because your soil will not yield its crops, nor will the trees of the land yield their fruit . . . I will send wild animals against you, and they will rob you of your children, destroy your cattle and make you so few in number that your roads will be deserted . . . I will bring the sword upon you to avenge the breaking of the covenant.

When you withdraw into your cities, I will send a plague among you, and you will be given into enemy hands . . . I will lay waste the land, so that your enemies who live there will be appalled. I will scatter you among the nations . . . Your land will be laid waste, and your cities will lie in ruins. Then the land will enjoy its sabbath years all the time that it lies desolate and you are in the country of your enemies; then the land will rest and enjoy its sabbaths. All the time that it lies desolate, the land will have the rest it did not have during the sabbaths you lived in it' (Lev. 26:19–35).

It is interesting to note God's insistence that the land would enjoy its sabbath, one way or another. If his people disobeyed his commands and failed to allow the land this sabbath rest then God would impose it by removing them from the land. The sabbath years came to represent the spirit of the Jubilee programmes. Everything about the Jubilee programmes is about giving rest or *shabbat*. A year's holiday obviously gives *shabbat* to the land, the servants, slaves and animals. But when debts are cancelled and slaves are set free, when loans are given without interest and the poor can glean from the edges of the harvest fields, the poor, the oppressed and those who are weary are being given *shabbat* as well. In other words, sabbath is not just about cessation of work for ourselves, it is also about the active giving of *shabbat* to others.

Jesus understood this when he healed the sick on the Sabbath. When asked by the Pharisees if it is lawful to heal on the Sabbath, he answered 'it is lawful to do good on the Sabbath' (Mt. 12:12) and healed the man with a shrivelled hand. He was giving real *shabbat* to this man who has been oppressed by sickness. No wonder he was able to make the invitation: 'Come to me, all you who are weary and burdened, and I will give you rest [*shabbat*]. Take my yoke upon you and learn from me, for I am gentle and humble in heart, and you will find rest [*shabbat*] for your souls' (Mt. 11:28).

In Gen 2:3, when God finished his work and rested on the seventh day, it says that 'God blessed the seventh day and made it holy, because on it he rested [*shabbat*] from all the work of creating that he had done.' Because God rested and enjoyed *shabbat* he wants his creation to also enter into his *shabbat*. Those who do not observe the *shabbat* and exploit their servants will meet with his judgement. But those who give *shabbat* to the weary and oppressed, both economic and spiritual, will receive his blessings. It was to be a day of equality in which all, high and low alike were entitled to rest.

Tied to the idea of *shabbat* is the concept of *shalom* (peace). Without *shabbat*, there can be no *shalom*. Where there is oppression, exploitation and injustice, there can be no peace. When the poor do not have a sabbath year and are unable to return to their land and their houses and sit under their vine and fig trees, there can be no *shalom*. Failure to observe the sabbath year meant the presence of ecological and human exploitation, a lack of justice and compassion for the oppressed poor. It was un-holy in that fellow Israelites were being denied the *shabbat* intended by God. There was also the absence of *shalom*. No wonder then God's declaration of punishment by taking the people away into exile for their disobedience.

From Judges to Kings

As ancient Israel transitioned from a nomadic to a settled agricultural society in Canaan, they were ruled by judges who were appointed by God on a non-stipendiary basis. They were based on the leadership style and model of Moses and Joshua, ruling the nation in a charismatic but de-centralised way. The nation was after all at this time a loose coalition of twelve tribes, each with their own interests and local government through the kinship structure. There was no centralised government to speak of.

In times of relative peace judges functioned as arbiters between the people, pronouncing judgement in matters of dispute. In times of national crises and war, they acted as national leaders to rally the nation against their common enemies. The role of the judges was, however, strictly limited. Significantly, during this early period in Israel's history, God was still recognised as the ultimate Judge (cf. Judg. 11:27). He was the King, and his rule was absolute.

Judges ruled Israel for approximately 150 years from the time of the initial settlement until Israel established a monarchy, a development that represented a significant and catastrophic shift in the economic and social foundations on which the nation was founded.

Although the Jubilee programmes themselves may not have been observed during the period of the judges, what might be called Jubilee principles (God's other laws and institutions regarding land ownership and family life) appear to have governed the economy and social structure. The story of Ruth, which we considered in the previous chapter, illustrates how much importance was attached to family control of land and property. Boaz was careful to follow the Jubilee legislation explicitly and approached the nearest kinsman (*goel*) to ask him if he would buy back the land that had belonged to Ruth's late father-in-law. When this kinsman refused, knowing that marriage to Ruth was also expected, Boaz willingly took this duty upon himself. The laws on gleaning also appeared to have been observed.

Eventually, however, the Israelites tired of the rule of the judges. This was a turbulent and chaotic period in the nation's history and a constant refrain was 'in those days Israel had no king; everyone did as he saw fit [or 'what was right in his own eyes']' (Judg. 21:25). After forty years of wandering, the nation had changed from a nomadic to a settled agricultural people. After another 150 years, the nation would transition from judges to kings, a move that would change forever the nature and structure of Israel.

1 Samuel 8:4 records how the elders of Israel gathered together and went to see Samuel, who had handed over his position as judge to his two sons. They told Samuel that they wanted a king because his sons were not ruling righteously. Although it was true that his sons were corrupt, having a king would not necessarily make things any better: kings were traditionally succeeded by their sons and therefore such corruption could easily be perpetuated and even harder to halt. Samuel was displeased and prayed to God who warned them of what would happen if they appointed a king:

'This is what the king who will reign over you will do: He will take your sons and make them serve with his chariots and horses, and they will run in front of his chariots. Some he will assign to be commanders of thousands and commanders of fifties, and others to plough his ground and reap his harvest, and still others to make weapons of war and equipment for his chariots. He will take your daughters to be perfumers and cooks and bakers. He will take the best of your fields and vineyards and olive groves and give them to his attendants. He will take a tenth of your grain and of your vintage and give it to his officials and attendants. Your men-servants and maidservants and the best of your cattle and donkeys he will take for his own use. He will take a tenth of your flocks, and you yourselves will become his slaves. When that day comes, you will cry out for relief from the king you have chosen, and the LORD will not answer you in that day' (1 Sam. 8:11–18).

But the people would not be deterred. Ignoring the warning, they revealed the real reason why they wanted a king: 'Then we shall be like all the other nations, with a king to lead us and to go out before us and to fight our battles' (1 Sam. 8:20). And there we have it. The whole foundation of the nationhood of Israel, which was based on trusting God as their King, was not what Israel wanted. They wanted an earthly king who could rule over them and lead them into battle – just like the other nations. The whole premise that Israel was to be different from the other nations in how they lived, their economics and government, right down to how they fought their enemies, would now be thrown out so that Israel could conform and be like the other nations. What in effect they were doing was rejecting their King and the way he ruled his kingdom. This was a serious matter and represented a watershed in Israel's history. In this we hear echoes of Jesus' words later on: 'We don't want this man to be our king' (Lk. 19:14).

Under God's kingship, Israel did not have a professional army. It was wholly voluntary, untrained and ill-prepared for combat. They were also not equipped with proper weapons of war. Furthermore God had some unorthodox battle strategies and methodologies that would test their faith (and patience) over and over again. In times of war, the judges would request the tribes to send their men on a voluntary basis and those who were willing to leave their farms, assembled with their agricultural and hunting tools as their weapons. This motley collection of farmers with their pitching forks, assembled against a fully-trained and equipped professional army on the other side, became a laughing stock with their enemies. It was the Israelite's equivalent of *Dad's Army*. God required that Israel should fight their battles with a voluntary army that was numerically inferior. When Gideon led the army against the Midianites (Judg. 7), God said that he had too many men! This was complying with the instructions given in Deuteronomy 20, sending home the faint-hearted and those who had recently married. Starting with 20,000, Gideon was told by God to send them all home leaving only 300 men. They were to be numerically inferior so that when the battle had been won, they would not boast that 'their own strength had saved them'. They would have to trust God for their deliverance in exactly the same way in which the Israelites had been delivered out of Egypt. Israel's army was also to be technologically inferior. No combat training, no army discipline and no proper weapons. Again God had instructed them: 'When you go to war against your enemies and see horses and chariots and an army greater than yours, do not be afraid of them, because the LORD your God, who brought you up out of Egypt, will be with you' (Deut. 20:1).

The lethal chariot was the most technologically advanced weapon of war in its day, the equivalent to the modern day Challenger 2 battle tank. Yet Israel was not to trust in chariots and had to destroy them whenever they captured some in battle (Josh. 11:6). God's style of battle is best exemplified by a small David with his sling and five pebbles against a fully-armed and armoured Goliath. His methodologies were unorthodox and unpredictable to say the least. These range from marching a group of musicians round the walls of Jericho, to Gideon and his men carrying trumpets and empty jars with candles ambushing their enemies at night! Despite this intentional inferiority and strange warfare methods, God led them to victory, again and again, when Israel trusted and obeyed his instructions.

Eventually, however, Israel had enough of this unconventional way of fighting. They wanted a professional army which they could count on and trust, and a king who could plan and lead them into battle. Where they would not have to fight with numerical and technological inferiority and put up with the strange warfare strategies of God which often left them with their hearts in their mouths. This is why they rejected God as King and wanted their own king – so that they would not have to trust and depend on him – and be like the other nations.

Reluctantly, God gave in to their demands but not before a solemn warning. Samuel, the prophet, warned that if they had a king, he would rule and exploit them in the same way as other kings (1 Sam. 8). In particular, God warned Israel that the following would happen:

- the king will make servants and slaves of your sons and daughters to work in his fields and kitchens and of course to serve in his army as professional soldiers;

- your sons will be conscripted to the fight in battle;
- a military command structure will be established, as will an arms industry producing lethal weaponry;
- there will be a land grab by the king for your best fields, vineyards and olive groves;
- the king will levy a tithe (10 per cent) tax on your grain, vines, donkeys and your flocks;
- the king will take your menservants and maidservants.

The bottom line was that Israel would become slaves of the king. Is this a price worth paying? The Jubilee programmes ensured that the land was equally distributed among the people. Now we will see land, and therefore capital, concentrated in the hands of the king and the royal palace cronies. The king will abuse his position because power always corrupts in the end. He will not be like Moses and Joshua, who were servant leaders. The king will lord it over his subjects and grab whatever and whoever he fancies because ultimate authority rests with him. Israel will become slaves (again) and lose their freedom as private citizens.

One change that would significantly impact the nation was the introduction of the income tax. Under the judges, there was no centralised taxation system in place. The Israelites were required to pay a tithe from their fields and flocks, but as we have seen earlier, this was given to the tabernacle and was used to feed the priests as well as the poor. The tax that would be exacted by the king would be used instead to support himself, his royal palaces, his professional army and his army of attendants, administrators and advisors. As soon as a centralised government and a professional army are established, taxes would have to be collected to support the monarchical structure. This was to prove a hugely expensive and catastrophic change. Israel would become like the other nations in more ways than it had originally wanted.

God's Kingdom

We should pause at this point to ask the question: what kind of economic society did God want for Israel based on our understanding thus far? I believe we can state the following features:

- *Private ownership*
  It was God's original intention that each family should own their own plot of land. Private ownership prevents the concentration of wealth, power and influence in fewer and fewer hands. Land was the asset or capital with which each family could create wealth and provide for their physical needs. Ultimately, it was a gift from God to each family, given to them with the responsibility of stewardship as God's tenants (Lev. 25:23). Whenever we talk of ownership we must not lose sight of the fact that all ownership in truth belongs to God (Ex. 19:5; Ps. 24:1).

- *Social security system based on kinship*
  The solidarity ('Israel is one') is centred on the extended family, clan and tribe who have the responsibilities for each other as blood relatives. When this kinship structure breaks down, the safety net for preventing people from falling into poverty collapses. Invariably then the state has to step in to provide a social security system for the poor funded, of course, out of taxation.

- *Corrective mechanisms to re-balance economic disparities at regular intervals*
  Here we are primarily thinking of the Jubilee programmes. From a political perspective, widening economic inequalities inevitably result in civil unrest. For political and social stability, the gap between the rich and poor cannot be too large. Otherwise the disaffected and marginalised, with no stake in the economy, will turn to violent means to address the inequalities. So the Jubilee programmes were not only valuable as

expressions of loving your neighbour and *shalom*, but were necessary as mechanisms for stable nationhood.

- *An independent judiciary*
  Even with the introduction of the monarchy, the roles of kings and prophets/priests were kept separate. Whilst the kings led the nation to war, the judges, prophets and priests had the responsibilities for moral and spiritual leadership, for ensuring that the Law was observed. It was the prophets in particular who spoke out against corruption and unfaithfulness in the nation. Sometimes the prophets had to speak out against the corruption of the kings themselves as with Elijah and King Ahab (1 Kgs. 21:17–19) and Nathan and King David (2 Sam. 12). An independent judiciary where no one is above the law is a prerequisite for justice. Judges and rulers who dispense justice must not be corrupt or accept bribes, and must defend the cause of the poor, fatherless and widows without fear or favour (2 Chr. 19:5–8; Amos 5:10–12).

- *Local government based on kinship structure*
  As we have just seen, the expensive monarchical system was not part of God's original intention for the nation. A low-cost, de-centralised government administration was what God had envisaged. When power is centralised and concentrated in a few hands, there is a tendency for abuse. Given humanity's fallen nature, there are few who can handle absolute power without being corrupted by it. And we shall see some examples of this abuse when we look at the injustices perpetrated by the kings.

- *Volunteer army*
  Every nation needs to be able to defend its borders against invaders. So it is that the greatness of a nation is measured by the size of its army. But with God as the Lord of hosts, that is the Commander-in-Chief, and Israel's unorthodox military strategy of *intentional inferiority*, no professional army or expensive military weapons were needed. Hence in the period

of the judges, Israel had a non-existent military budget. The nation under God would be able to defeat their enemies using ragtag volunteer farmers so that they could truly say 'In God we trust'.

- *No income tax*
  Israel did not need an Inland Revenue department to collect taxes. Only with the introduction of the kingship did Israel need taxes to run its expensive royal palaces, government bureaucracy and defence. Israel was intended as a tax haven. With no centralised bureaucracy and army to support, the Israelites did not have to pay taxes. Now, this really is utopia! With more money in their pockets, they would have been better able to provide for their families, clan relatives and neighbours.

The outworking of such principles in a nation would have been exciting to see. We would have seen a free market but compassionate society built on strong families, where the poor were cared for, and one which was run by a small de-centralised government with little bureaucracy and no taxation. We would have seen a society where people loved their neighbours in practical ways. What a missed opportunity then for Israel.

Injustices Under the Kings

Israel had been warned that the way of life they had known would be completely overthrown. Wealth and power would no longer be equally distributed amongst the people but would be concentrated in the hands of the king and those close to him. The king would claim rights of ownership over the land and the people. He would introduce military service, forced labour and taxation. In short, the king would assume the role and rights of God.

It was not long before there was evidence of this pride in the monarchy. Saul, Israel's very first king, was a humble man when

Samuel first anointed him – 'But am I not a Benjamite, from the smallest tribe of Israel, and is not my clan the least of all the clans of the tribe of Benjamin?' (1 Sam. 9:21) – but over the course of his reign his heart became proud: 'Early in the morning Samuel got up and went to meet Saul, but he was told, "Saul has gone to Carmel. There he has set up a monument in his own honour"' (1 Sam. 15:12). Saul had begun to seek for himself the glory that was God's alone. He also made his officials wealthy by giving them land (1 Sam. 22:7), presumably seizing it from its original owners just as God had warned the king would do.

God finally rejected Saul in favour of David, Israel's most famous king. David began the process of the centralization of power in earnest. He made Jerusalem the new capital of the kingdom and it became his personal property. But it was during the reign of Solomon, his son, that this process gained its real momentum. Taxes were levied in the form of grain and cattle to meet the needs of the royal household (1 Kgs. 4:22,23), and forced labour was used to build the temple and the King's palace (1 Kgs. 5:13–18; 9:15–23). Life for the people of Israel was starting to resemble God's warning in 1 Samuel 8. The average peasant farmer was not free merely to work his land and care for his family – he was also beholden to the king, who was placing heavy demands on his time and his labour.

As Solomon grew old he became less devoted to God and started to worship foreign gods. Because of his unfaithfulness, God tore all but the tribe and territory of Judah away from Solomon's son, Rehoboam. The remainder fell into the hands of Jeroboam, one of Solomon's officials. From that time onwards there were two kingdoms – Judah, the Southern Kingdom, and Israel, the Northern Kingdom. Economic injustices and corruption continued to thrive in both. God's Jubilee values were regularly abused.

An important illustration of this kind of abuse is found in 1 Kgs. 21. This chapter tells the story of Ahab, the King of Israel, who decided that he wanted to have the vineyard of a man called Naboth because it was close to his palace. He approached Naboth, offering either to pay him the price of the vineyard or to give him a better vineyard in exchange. Naboth's reply revealed a deeply-held belief that the land should remain within his family, in accordance with God's law: 'The LORD forbid that I should give you the inheritance of my fathers' (1 Kgs. 21:3). Ahab reported Naboth's reaction to his wife Jezebel whose response was interesting: 'Is this how you act as king over Israel?' (v. 7). In other words, if you were a real king, like those in the other nations, you would simply grab what you want. She then told her feeble husband to leave the matter to her. Jezebel proceeded to have Naboth falsely charged with blasphemy. Naboth was executed and Ahab was able to seize his vineyard. But God rebuked Ahab through the prophet Elijah: 'Have you not murdered a man and seized his property?' (v. 19) and told him that he would die an ignominious death. He also punished him by cutting off all of his male descendants, thereby terminating his extended family. This was what Ahab had done to Naboth's family.

It is clear from this story that, even under the kings, the Israelites continued to regard permanent ownership of land as a fundamental right. The story demonstrates the restrictions placed on royalty – they were not entitled to seize private land in defiance of the Jubilee regulations. Ahab and Jezebel had to go to great lengths to enforce their will.

The Role of the Prophets

The story of Naboth's vineyard provides an illustration of how God used his prophets to denounce injustice and warn his people of the punishments they would suffer for exploiting the poor. Economic oppression and corruption was, in fact, a central theme in the pronouncements of all the prophets, showing just how much the plight of the poor mattered to God.

A large number of the prophets' attacks were directed at unrighteous kings, of which there were many. A typical example of the kind of accusation levelled at these kings is found in Jeremiah 22, a chapter that is worth studying in its entirety. We will just quote a handful of verses here:

> 'Woe to him who builds his palace by unrighteousness,
> his upper rooms by injustice,
> making his countrymen work for nothing,
> not paying them for their labour.
> He says, "I will build myself a great palace
> with spacious upper rooms."
> So he makes large windows in it,
> panels it with cedar
> And decorates it in red.
>
> Does it make you a king to have more and more cedar?
> Did not your father have food and drink?
> He did what was right and just,
> so all went well with him.
> He defended the cause of the poor and needy,
> and so all went well.
> Is that not what it means to know me?' declares the LORD
> (Jer. 22:13–16).

Notice that knowing God is defined by Jeremiah as defending the cause of the poor and needy. Faith is not just mental beliefs but acts of mercy as well. However, it was not only kings who were guilty of injustice and exploitation. The corrupt actions of legislators and officials were also denounced:

> Woe to those who make unjust laws,
> to those who issue oppressive decrees,
> to deprive the poor of their rights

and withhold justice from the oppressed of my people,
making widows their prey
and robbing the fatherless (Is. 10:1,2).

Also under attack were wealthy landowners who showed disregard for the Jubilee values of fairness and wealth distribution, seeking instead to acquire ever greater amounts of land and property at the expense of others:

Woe to you who add house to house
and join field to field
till no space is left
and you live alone in the land (Is. 5:8).

Woe to those who plan iniquity,
to those who plot evil on their beds!
At morning's light they carry it out
because it is in their power to do it.
They covet fields and seize them,
and houses, and take them.
They defraud a man of his home,
a fellow-man of his inheritance
(Mich. 2:1,2).

The prophet Ezekiel decried the fact that God's people had turned their backs on the principle of interest-free loans and would do literally anything to obtain money: 'In you [Jerusalem] men accept bribes to shed blood; you take usury and excessive interest and make unjust gain from your neighbours by extortion' (Ezek. 22:12).

And the prophet Amos condemned the myriad ways in which commercial trading had become a degraded activity, shaped by selfish and exploitative attitudes. The picture he paints is of a society alarmingly like our own:

Hear this, you who trample the needy
and do away with the poor of the land,
saying,
'When will the New Moon be over
that we may sell grain,
and the Sabbath be ended
that we may market wheat?' –
skimping the measure,
boosting the price
and cheating with dishonest scales,
buying the poor with silver
and the needy for a pair of sandals,
selling even the sweepings with the wheat (Amos 8:4–6).

The overall impression is of a society driven overwhelmingly by selfishness and greed. The concept of solidarity is absent. It is each man for himself. The Israelites had evidently lost sight of the values that God had sought to instil in his people during their wilderness years. The Jubilee principles of trust in God, moderation with respect to one's own needs, and generosity towards the needs of one's neighbour, had been completely abandoned.

Tragically, it was possible to be religious and yet turn a blind eye to the injustices around. Temple worship and even fasting continued to be practised by the devout, but these same worshippers were the very oppressors of the poor. They exploited their workers, they ignored the hungry and allowed injustice to go unchallenged. For them, social justice had nothing to do with their faith. In their minds, creed and conduct were disconnected. Isaiah and Amos had some strong words for these religious people who did nothing to alleviate the injustices around them:

'For day after day they seek me out; they seem eager to know my ways,
as if they were a nation that does what is right . . .

"Why have we fasted," they say, "and you have not seen it?

Why have we humbled ourselves, and you have not noticed?"

Yet on the day of your fasting, you do as you please and exploit all your workers . . .

Is not this the kind of fasting I have chosen:

to loose the chains of injustice

and untie the cords of the yoke,

To set the oppressed free and break every yoke?

Is it not to share your food with the hungry and to provide the poor wanderer with shelter –

when you see the naked, to clothe him, and not to turn away from your own flesh and blood?' (Is. 58:2–7).

'I hate, I despise your religious feasts; I cannot stand your assemblies.

Even though you bring me burnt offerings and grain offerings, I will not accept them.

Though you bring choice fellowship offerings, I will have no regard for them.

Away with the noise of your songs! I will not listen to the music of your harps.

But let justice roll on like a river, righteousness like a never-failing stream!' (Amos 5:21–24).

God literally became sick with the people's religiosity – their worship music, burnt offerings and religious festivals. He couldn't even listen to their songs of praise. They honoured God with their lips, but their hearts were far away from him. They sang their worship songs, and yet there were members of their congregation going hungry. They fasted, but they bought 'the poor with silver and the needy for a pair of sandals' (Amos 8:6). This was religion without reality, faith without works, words without actions. No wonder God warned, '"In that day," declares the Sovereign LORD, "the songs in the temple will turn to wailing. Many, many bodies – flung everywhere! Silence!"' (Amos 8:3).

The Israelites' fate was now certain. Just as their craving had led to their destruction at Kibroth Hattaavah (Num. 11:34), so once again their destruction was sure. In 722 BC the Northern Kingdom fell to the Assyrians, and just a little over a century later, in 587 BC, the Southern Kingdom fell to the Babylonians. Significantly, the final straw leading to Jerusalem's downfall was an act of disobedience concerning the Jubilee laws. In apparent submission to these laws, King Zedekiah made a proclamation of liberty, freeing all slaves. A combination of military and religious motives lay behind this act, however. The nation was at war with Nebuchadnezzar of Babylon who was about to lay siege to Jerusalem. Zedekiah needed more soldiers. He also hoped that God would be pleased with the release of slaves, and would come to his aid. The two goals fitted nicely together. But the owners cancelled the agreement and took back the slaves in direct defiance of the original covenant which stated that they would not be enslaved again. Using Jeremiah as his mouthpiece, God made plain what the consequence would be:

'You have not proclaimed freedom for your fellow countrymen. So I now proclaim "freedom" for you, declares the LORD – "freedom" to fall by the sword, plague and famine . . . I will hand Zedekiah king of Judah and his officials over to their enemies who seek their lives, to the army of the king of Babylon, which has withdrawn from you. I am going to give the order, declares the LORD, and I will bring them back to this city. They will fight against it, take it and burn it down. And I will lay waste the towns of Judah so that no-one can live there' (Jer. 34:17–22).

The people's fate was sealed. They had tested God's patience too far. On a previous occasion, during the reign of Hezekiah, God had spared Jerusalem from destruction by Sennacherib, the King of Assyria. At that time he had showered them with Jubilee blessings as a sign of his deliverance and provision (Is. 37:30, cf. Lev. 25:11).

But now God was setting his people free to experience the consequences of their disobedience. Their corrupt economy was destroyed. All property titles were obliterated and there would be no way to reclaim inherited properties (cf. Ezek. 7:10–14). The land was able to enjoy its sabbath rests, just as God had promised: 'all the time of its desolation it rested, until the seventy years were completed in fulfilment of the word of the LORD spoken by Jeremiah' (2 Chr. 36:21). What a tragedy for a new nation that had started out so well, and on such great foundations for a just and compassionate society.

God the Redeemer

The role of the prophets was not merely to denounce sin and express God's judgement, however. It was also to extend hope to the poor and oppressed and to those who kept faith with God. During the pre-exilic period, the prophets' words offered comfort to those who were oppressed by their fellow Israelites. Their vindication, they were told, was not far away. During the post-exilic period, when God's punishment had fallen on his people for their sins, God in his mercy used the prophets to assure his people that he had not abandoned them for ever. They would not always suffer oppression at the hands of their enemies. Once again, vindication was coming. The assurances of the prophets were echoed by those of the psalmists – God was on the side of the poor and victimised, and would avenge the injustices done to them (cf. Ps. 94; 103:6; 146:7–9).

Through their pronouncements, the prophets were therefore responsible for a gradual but very significant shift in the people's understanding of the Jubilee. As more and more people turned away from God's laws, the Jubilee ceased to be portrayed primarily as the action of God's people carried out in obedience to him. Instead it started to be depicted more and more as God's action on behalf of his people.

Isaiah, in particular, was responsible for this shift in under-standing. On numerous occasions he spoke of God's vengeance on behalf of the oppressed and of a future King who would restore justice – see for example chapters 28, 32, 42 and 59. Elsewhere he was even more explicit, making direct references to Israel's failure to observe the Jubilee and of God's decision to assume the role of Redeemer (*goel*) on behalf of his people:

> The spirit of the Sovereign LORD is on me,
> because the LORD has anointed me
> to preach good news to the poor.
> He has sent me to bind up the broken-hearted,
> to proclaim freedom for the captives
> and release from darkness for the prisoners,
> to proclaim the year of the LORD's favour
> and the day of vengeance of our God (Is. 61:1,2).

> For the day of vengeance was in my heart,
> and the year of my redemption has come.
> I looked, but there was no-one to help,
> I was appalled that no-one gave support;
> so my own arm worked salvation for me,
> and my own wrath sustained me (Is. 63:4,5).

Isaiah was not using the word 'prisoners' in the criminal sense. He was referring to people who were shackled by economic and social conditions from which there was no escape. The Redeemer would take direct, forceful action to correct these injustices and to free Israel from its oppressors. The task of bringing freedom and justice was now firmly established as the activity of God. The word translated as 'freedom' in verse 2 of Isaiah 61 is *'deror'* in Hebrew, the same term that is used in Leviticus 25 to refer to the Jubilee proclamation of liberty.

The prophets used actions as well as words to teach the people about God's redemptive character. During the siege of Jerusalem, shortly before its downfall, Jeremiah was approached by his cousin and asked to buy a field. As the nearest relative, it was Jeremiah's right and duty to buy it, and he did so. Due to the impending war and the location of the property (the enemy would march right across it), the redemption price was very small. The transaction was a prophetic act, however. It was a sign to the Israelites that although the land was to be taken away from them, they would one day be in possession of it again. God would redeem it. He was the consummate kinsman redeemer.

The Return from Exile

Hope was hard to hold on to, in spite of the prophets' reassurances. The kingdoms of Israel and Judah were now no more. Their monarchies had ceased to exist, and the people had been scattered. Even the temple had been destroyed. The period in exile was a desolate time for the people of Israel. In spite of the prophets' assurances that God would restore them to their land, it is clear from the book of Lamentations that the feelings of loss and despair, and even humiliation, were at times overwhelming.

But God had not forgotten his people. The Babylonians, who had captured Judah, were themselves defeated by the Persians in 538 BC. God then moved the heart of the Persian king, Cyrus, to issue a decree allowing the Israelites to return to Jerusalem and rebuild the temple. After just fifty years in exile, the Israelites began to return to their homeland.

God was giving his people the opportunity to make a fresh start. But they had to do things differently this time. During the period of exile, Ezekiel received a vision, showing him God's perfect plan for the land and the temple (Ezek. 40–45). The vision had a dual meaning – it referred both to the Israelites' imminent return from exile and to the far-distant future when all things would be made new (many aspects of the vision are picked up again in the book of Revelation). It therefore had both an eschatological (end time) and a present-day significance, and the difference between the two was not entirely clear. What was clear, however, was that the old system of government and land distribution was not acceptable. Land was to be divided up fairly and was not to be confiscated. Justice and fairness were to be the order of the day (cf. Ezek. 45:7–10).

The early chapters of the book of Ezra record the first actions of the Israelites when they returned to Israel. In spite of their fear of the people around them, they built an altar and made sacrifices and offerings in accordance with the Law of Moses. The foundations of the new temple were laid and the Israelites sang their praises to God. It was a good start – the worship of God was being made a priority. This initial zeal must have gradually worn off, for eighteen years later the prophet Haggai rebuked the Israelites for having neglected the work on the temple, preferring instead to build luxurious houses for themselves. It was true that they had faced opposition, but this was not accepted as an adequate reason by the prophet: 'Is it a time for you yourselves to be living in your panelled houses, while this house remains a ruin?' (Hag. 1:4).

The people had not been giving the first fruits of their time and their labour to God – they had been seeking instead to first meet their own needs, revealing a fundamental lack of trust in God's provision. Although they responded to Haggai's challenge and completed the work on the temple, it was not long before God raised up another prophet to rebuke them. Once again they were cheating him, this time by bringing defective animals to the altar, and by withholding a proportion of their tithe:

'When you bring injured, crippled or diseased animals and offer them as sacrifices, should I accept them from your hands?' says the LORD. 'Cursed is the cheat who has an acceptable male in his

flock and vows to give it, but then sacrifices a blemished animal to
the LORD. For I am a great king,' says the LORD Almighty, 'and my
name is to be feared among the nations' (Mal. 1:13,14).

'You are under a curse – the whole nation of you – because you are
robbing me. Bring the whole tithe into the storehouse, that there
may be food in my house. Test me in this,' says the LORD Almighty,
'and see if I will not throw open the floodgates of heaven and pour
out so much blessing that you will not have room enough for it. I
will prevent pests from devouring your crops, and the vines in
your fields will not cast their fruit,' says the LORD Almighty (Mal.
3:9–11).

It was the priests who were blamed for the blemished sacrifices,
for in presenting such offerings to God they had shown contempt
for his name. They had failed to instruct the people in the ways
of truth and had instead caused many to stumble. Malachi 3:9–11
refers to the tithing or sabbath year laws where God had promised that the harvest of the intervening years would be so good
that there would be excess, enough for several years so that 'you
will not have room enough for it'. Provided the people brought
their tithe, and the whole of it. In withholding a part of their tithe,
they were depriving the poor and also saying they did not trust
God to provide for their needs according to his promises. This
well-known passage has often been used by the prosperity teachers to 'convince and condemn' their members about tithing. But
note that the tithe is largely meant for the poor not the priests and
pastors. We should also note that the context of the passage is
God's judgement against 'sorcerers, adulterers and perjurers,
against those who defraud labourers of their wages, who oppress
the widows and the fatherless, and deprive aliens of justice, but
do not fear me' (Mal. 3:5). God's judgement is not just against
those who commit sexual and spiritual sins. He will punish those
who commit economic sins against the vulnerable as well.

Malachi sums up the prevailing attitude amongst the people: 'You have said, "It is futile to serve God. What did we gain by carrying out his requirements and going about like mourners before the LORD Almighty? But now we call the arrogant blessed. Certainly the evildoers prosper, and even those who challenge God escape"' (Mal. 3:14,15).

It was during the period of Malachi's ministry that Nehemiah returned to Jerusalem. During his time in exile, he had been taken into the service of the King of Persia, but when news reached him that the wall of Jerusalem was lying in ruins he became anxious to return to his homeland. Sensitive to his distress, the king gave him permission to go. But when Nehemiah returned he discovered that the state of the wall was not the only problem facing the exiles. They also faced serious economic problems:

- Their children were being sold into slavery in order to get food.
- Their fields and vineyards were heavily mortgaged, leaving them without resources to redeem their own children.
- They had to pay exorbitant taxes to the king.

Nehemiah was angered to discover that the people's creditors were not the foreign authorities but their fellow countrymen (Neh. 5:7). The people were destroying each other through usury. Significantly, Nehemiah invoked the Jubilee principle of debt cancellation to resolve the crisis (Neh. 10:31). The people responded immediately. Land was restored and funds were released for the redemption of children and the purchase of food.

Nehemiah understood that the exile was due in part to the failure of Israel to observe the Jubilee. Accordingly, it became his mission not only to rebuild the wall of Jerusalem but also to rekindle the faith of his people. Once the wall had been completed, the scribe Ezra read from the Book of the Law, just as Moses had instructed the priests to do every sabbath year once they had entered the Promised Land (see Deut. 31:9–12). The Israelites then made a corporate confession of their sins, acknowledging the consequences of their choices and actions (Neh. 9:36,37). Finally, they made a binding agreement to follow once again the commands and laws that God had given them, including the requirement to give tithes and to observe the sabbath year by allowing the land to rest and cancelling debts.

It is at approximately this point (circa 440 BC) that we reach the end of Old Testament biblical history. What is known of the intertestamental period is derived chiefly from other historical sources. The Persian empire finally collapsed in 331 BC to be replaced by the Greek empire. This empire also fell in 63 BC, and was replaced by the Roman empire. It was, of course, during the time of the Roman occupation that Christ was born.

How successfully did the Israelites continue to follow Jubilee principles during this intertestamental period? We gain a small insight from the story of the Maccabean revolt (from 175 BC to 134 BC), recorded in the apocryphal book 1 Maccabees.[1] Its account of the siege of Bethzur suggests that the sabbath year was being observed as late as the second century before Christ, although there is no evidence that this was on a regular basis:

> The royal army moved up to encounter them before Jerusalem, and the king [King Antiochus of Greece] began to blockade Judaea and Mount Zion. He granted peace terms to the people of Bethzur, who evacuated the town; it lacked store of provisions to withstand a siege, since the land was enjoying a sabbatical year. Having occupied Bethzur, the king stationed a garrison there to hold it. He besieged the sanctuary for a long time, erecting firing platforms

---

[1] 1 and 2 Maccabees are accepted as canonical books of the Bible by the Catholic and Orthodox churches, but not by Protestant denominations. Their usefulness as historical texts is, however, undisputed. 1 Maccabees tells the story of the conquest of Palestine by the Greeks and the Jewish revolt against Greek rule.

and siege-engines, fire-throwers and ballistas, scorpions to dis-
charge arrows, and catapults. The defenders countered these by
constructing their own engines, and were thus able to prolong
their resistance. But they had no stocks of provisions, because it
was the seventh year, and those who had taken refuge in Judaea
from the pagans had eaten up the last of their reserves (1 Macc.
6:48–54, *The Jerusalem Bible*).

The Israelites were evidently still observing the sabbath year at
the time of the Greek conquest. It was certainly true that, under
Persian rule, the Israelites had been able to enjoy a measure of
autonomy in religious and social matters. Under the Greeks,
however, a process of Hellenisation began whereby the external
imposition of Greek culture, language and religion led to a widespread internalisation of Greek ideals and values. There were dis-
senters, of course (most notably Judas, one of the leaders of the
Maccabean revolt), but many of the Israelites accepted the new
Hellenised way of life. Eventually the Greek empire gave way to
the Roman empire, and in 37 BC Herod was appointed King of
Judea by the Romans. Herod had only tenuous Jewish credentials
and was a great promoter of Graeco-Roman culture. During his
reign, he completed a number of huge building projects in honour of the Emperor and Roman culture – the harbour at Caesarea,
various temples to Roman gods, amphitheatres, theatres and hip-
podromes. He also carried out extensive rebuilding work on the
temple, but his motivation was doubtless more tactical than spiritual. In order to control them successfully, Herod needed to pay
lip service to the values of the Jews. In truth, he was a ruthless
despot, ambitious only for his own self-aggrandisement.

By the time the New Testament era dawned, the economic and
political life of the nation was therefore entirely different to what
it had been at the time of the Israelites' original settlement in the
land. Many aspects of the Jubilee programmes and principles had
consequently become obsolete. The majority of people were now

landless, dispossessed and urbanised. They had to pay taxes to a foreign ruler, Caesar. Many of them had debts, but there was no one in authority to announce a Jubilee and organise their cancellation.

It was against this social backdrop that Jesus was born.

5

Jesus and the Jubilee

To recap, the story so far is that after leaving Egypt as slaves, the Israelites led a nomadic existence for forty years in the wilderness. On entering the Promised Land, they became a settled agricultural society under the judges and the kings only later to become slaves a second time in Persia. (Even for the brave remnants who returned from exile, the land of Israel during the New Testament times would be occupied by foreign armies and for the majority of the people, their land would have been lost for ever.) Injustice and economic disparity had clearly increased during the reign of the kings because the Jubilee provisions were ignored and also because of the abuse of power by the royal palaces. During this time, the Jubilee was not completely forgotten. Instead it became a picture of the future kingdom which will be ushered in when *Mashiach* (messiah) comes. While the period under the judges, Saul and David was chaotic, the Israelites nevertheless remembered them as 'the golden years' when they could farm their own fields, live in their houses and sit under their vines and fig trees. Compared to the time when they were ruled by bad kings or when they were in captivity, those were idyllic times.

The prophets took up the theme of this future hope of a Jubilee kingdom of justice and *shalom*. This utopian society would only happen when *Mashiach* came to deliver them from their oppressors and at the same time re-introduce Jubilee. *Mashiach* would be like Moses (Deut. 18:15,18) and would bring deliverance as well as give new laws, written in their hearts this time, not on tablets of stone (Jer. 31:33; 2 Cor. 3:3). As to when, the prophets said that Elijah would come again (Mal. 4:5) and he would precede *Mashiach*. This future hope is best summarised by the prophet Zechariah: '"In that day each of you will invite his neighbour to sit under his vine and fig-tree," declares the LORD Almighty' (Zech. 3:10). This is Isaiah's 'year of the LORD's favour' (Is. 61:2; 49:8–26), the Jubilee year when everyone returned to their own plot of land and houses and were able again to sit under their vines and fig-trees in *shalom*.

Another thing that would happen when *Mashiach* came is that he would prepare a great feast or banquet: 'On this mountain the LORD Almighty will prepare a feast of rich food for all peoples, a banquet of aged wine – the best of meats and the finest of wines' (Is. 25:6). As we have seen, the Israelites spent a lot of time 'eating and drinking' because to 'eat bread' is to have fellowship and share in *shalom*. *Mashiach* will prepare a great feast to celebrate the kingdom's coming and everyone is invited including the poor, fatherless, widows and foreigners. By the time of the New Testament, the Pharisees understood that they were going to be present at the banquet as God's chosen people but they were not expecting the social outcasts and Gentile foreigners to be there, too.

The Bible can in fact be viewed as a continuum of 'eating and drinking' – from the story of Adam in Genesis, through to the sacrifices and festivals in Leviticus, to Jesus eating and drinking with sinners, the early disciples having meals 'from house to house' and feeding the poor, to the marriage feast of the Lamb in Revelation. When a sheikh or emir invites people to a feast, he sends out a servant to call the guests at the proper time with the words: '*Tefuddulu, al'asha hader*' meaning 'Come, for the feast is ready.' The parable of the Great Dinner contains the same invitation (Lk. 14:17) and resonates with the marriage feast of the Lamb (Rev. 19:9; 22:17). The Jews had a saying: 'Blessed is the man who will eat at the feast in the kingdom of God' (Lk. 14:15). Blessed indeed is the one will be at *Mashiach's* banquet.

So who is this *Mashiach*? The best way to describe him is as a servant king. He will deliver Israel from their enemies and 'reign on David's throne and over his kingdom' (Is. 9:7). And yet this king comes in peace on a lowly donkey rather than a horse as a warrior (Zech. 9:9). Isaiah 42:1 calls him a servant but one who 'establishes justice on earth' (Is. 42:4). He will be a Saviour (Is. 62:11) and a Redeemer (Is. 60:16). And here the language of Jubilee, the redeemer kinsman (the *goel*) is used for *Mashiach* along with the idea of shalom and justice.

With the expectation of *Mashiach* as a king, the language of Jubilee also changes to that of the kingdom. Through their own experience of kingship and that of the surrounding nations, Israel would have been familiar with kings and their kingdoms. This future hope expressed in kingdom language however was already there at Sinai: 'Now if you obey me fully and keep my covenant, then out of all nations you will be my treasured possession. Although the whole earth is mine, you will be for me a kingdom of priests and a holy nation' (Ex. 19:5,6).

God's intention all along was to form a holy nation or kingdom. But in regards to the Jubilee laws, how will these be implemented in this 'kingdom of priests and holy nation'? After all, their political and economic situation is vastly different. Israel is now a country occupied by the Romans. It is a much more urbanised society than the time of the judges. The majority of the people are landless with many day labourers waiting for work each day. Without owning their land, most are unable to provide for their families. There was huge economic disparity, injustice was rife and poverty was endemic. How can Jubilee be implemented in such a society? What would the Jubilee kingdom look like?

We will turn now to *Yeshua the Mashiach* to see how he interpreted and re-activated Jubilee for his day. But before that we need to briefly mention John the Baptist.

Preparing the Way

When John the Baptist appeared, his role was to prepare the way for Jesus by giving the people 'the knowledge of salvation through the forgiveness of their sins' (Lk. 1:77). Like the prophets before him, he called the people to repentance: ' "What should we do then?' " the crowd asked. John answered, "The man with two tunics should share with him who has none, and the one who has food should do the same"' (Lk. 3:10,11).

Right away we see Jubilee generosity being advocated by John. Anyone with two of anything was to share it with the poor – from clothes and shoes to food. If everyone in the crowd who heard John returned home and acted on his words, there would have been a scene not dissimilar to the tithing year. As we have noted, some scholars have calculated that Jesus began his ministry in a literal Jubilee year. If true, then John's ministry occurred during a literal sabbath year.

> Tax collectors also came to be baptised. 'Teacher,' they asked, 'what should we do?'
> 'Don't collect any more than you are required to,' he told them.
> Then some soldiers asked him, 'And what should we do?'
> He replied, 'Don't extort money and don't accuse people falsely – be content with your pay' (Lk. 3:12–14).

The kind of repentance that John was preaching was explicitly tied up with Jubilee values of social holiness and justice. The command to love one's neighbour (Lev. 19:18) had concrete applications and essentially expressed itself in terms of meeting the needs of the poor. Love was to be worked out in terms of justice. The kind of repentance that John was seeking was not therefore a private affair. It was public and it was practical. It meant the restoration of *shalom*, which was fundamentally a social concept. For many of us today, the word repentance has lost this practical edge. Just as we tend to spiritualise our concept of holiness – making it a matter of personal devotion rather than a matter of social action – so we tend to spiritualise our concept of repentance, and ignore its social dimension. We forget that repentance is as much an action as it is an attitude. For John, the two were inseparably bound up with each other.

This is a consistent message throughout the Old Testament. Creed and conduct, belief and behaviour are inseparable. You cannot go to the temple to ask for God's forgiveness and then go out to perpetrate injustice by extortion and false accusation in order to extract bribes.

Jesus – the Bringer of Jubilee Good News

He went to Nazareth, where he had been brought up, and on the Sabbath day he went into the synagogue, as was his custom. And he stood up to read. The scroll of the prophet Isaiah was handed to him. Unrolling it, he found the place where it is written:

'The Spirit of the Lord is on me,
because he has anointed me
to preach good news to the poor.
He has sent me to proclaim freedom for the prisoners
and recovery of sight for the blind,
to release the oppressed,
to proclaim the year of the Lord's favour.'

Then he rolled up the scroll, gave it back to the attendant and sat down. The eyes of everyone in the synagogue were fastened on him, and he began by saying to them, 'Today this scripture is fulfilled in your hearing' (Lk. 4:16–21).

In the Nazareth Manifesto, Jesus clearly intended his ministry to be understood in terms of 'the year of the Lord's favour'. Whether or not this was a literal Jubilee year, there is little doubt that he was announcing a Jubilee. He claimed that 'this scripture has been fulfilled in your hearing'. But what does Jubilee mean for Jesus and how does he intend to implement it? After all, circumstances have changed since the Jubilee programmes were given. The existence of vast urbanised wealth and extensive Gentile land ownership makes the original implementation impractical. Besides, the Roman authorities would certainly have none of it. But Jesus is creative and innovative and we see him creating a form of Jubilee that was appropriate to the social and political conditions of his day. This is what we will now turn our attention to, looking at both his works and his words in Jubilee terms.

Jesus' Jubilee Actions

Common purse

When Jesus gathered around him the twelve disciples and started an itinerant ministry, they were accompanied and financially supported by a group of women. Prominent among these women were 'Mary (called Magdalene) from whom seven demons had come out; Joanna the wife of Chuza, the manager of Herod's household; Susanna; and many others. These women were helping to support them out of their own means' (Lk. 8:2,3). These women had been cured of evil spirits and disease and were committed to supporting this band of travelling preachers out of their own means. Joanna and her husband Chuza are evidence for the existence of disciples among the aristocracy. Mary, Joanna and Susanna were no doubt named because they became well known later on in the church.

It appears that Jesus and the group of disciples practised a common purse and shared what they had. This common purse was managed by Judas Iscariot (what grace!) and was used to buy food as well as to give to the poor (Jn. 13:29). Through this practice of holding a common purse, we see the foundations for the common life of the church after Pentecost. The disciples had already lived this way for three years with Jesus. By choosing this way of life, the Jesus community expressed Jubilee features of solidarity, social holiness, justice and *shalom*.

Given the change in the economic situation of the first century AD compared with Old Testament times, sharing a common purse was an effective way of expressing Jubilee. Everyone within this extended 'family' would be provided for on an equitable basis. No one had any need within this mobile Jubilee community.

He set the captives free

The people Jesus encountered were all bound and crippled in one way or another. In some cases, it was physically apparent – as with the leprous, the blind, the paralytic, the demon-possessed. In other cases, it was socially evident – as with the tax collectors and prostitutes. In still other cases, it may have been invisible to all but God who looked on the inside – as with the Pharisees.

In each case, the offer of Jesus was freedom from their captivity to sin, pride and sickness. As well as perfectly demonstrating the holistic nature of his ministry, his linking of these two made plain the interconnectedness of the material and spiritual dimensions of human existence.

'Some men brought to him a paralytic, lying on a mat. When Jesus saw their faith, he said to the paralytic, "Take heart, son; your sins are forgiven." (Mt. 9:2). The word translated 'forgiven' comes from the Greek verb *'aphiemi'*, a term used regularly in the New Testament to mean both to 'forgive' sins and to 'release' from debt. The Jubilee undertones are plain.

Freeing the captives was the touchstone and hallmark of Jesus' ministry. Its fullest expression came at the climax of Jesus' ministry, in his death on the cross: 'He himself bore our sins in his body on the tree, so that we might die to sins and live for righteousness' (1 Pet. 2:24). As we saw in Chapter 3, one of the roles of the kinsman redeemer (*goel*) was to buy back a family member who had sold himself into slavery or indentured service. Through his death on the cross, Jesus bought us back from slavery to sin and thereby performed the ultimate act of kinsman redemption. Through his death on the cross, Jesus also enacted a Jubilee – providing freedom from slavery, freedom from debt and the restoration of relationship with the family of God. The New Testament writers understood the significance of Christ's death from this Old Testament perspective:

> You are not your own; you were bought at a price (1 Cor. 6:19,20).

> In him we have redemption through his blood, the forgiveness of sins (Eph. 1:7).

> For you know that it was not with perishable things such as silver or gold that you were redeemed from the empty way of life handed down to you from your forefathers, but with the precious blood of Christ (1 Pet. 1:18,19).

The cross is, of course, the most powerful example of Jesus choosing to empty himself of his own personal wealth for the sake of community gain. In the desert, the devil had tempted him to jump from the highest point of the temple and be rescued by God's angels. The cross must surely have recalled that moment of temptation. But once again Jesus held firm. In the face of community need, he forsook the selfish option in order that the blessings of obedience might be distributed as widely as possible.

He fed the hungry

Matthew 14, Mark 6, Luke 9 and John 6 all record the occasion when a crowd of 5,000 men (plus women and children) came to hear Jesus preach. It got late and they had nothing to eat except five loaves and two fishes belonging to a little boy. Taking the loaves and the fishes, Jesus gave thanks for them, broke the loaves and distributed the food. Miraculously there was enough for everyone, and even some left over. It is the only miracle to be recorded in all four Gospels.

It is an incident that has both spiritual and material significance, and looks both forwards and backwards. On one level, the story foreshadows the Last Supper – Jesus breaking the bread and sharing it amongst his disciples. This bread, of course, represents his body, which is given for the world. Within this context, our hunger and our need are not physical but spiritual. Jesus himself encouraged his disciples to read a spiritual meaning into his feeding of the 5,000 by going on to state, 'I am the bread of life' (Jn. 6:35).

But there are also powerful echoes in this story of the miraculous provision of manna for the Israelites in the desert. Jesus was showing the people that he was willing and able to take care of their material needs. And there was a powerful lesson latent in the way he did it. By putting one person's (in this case, a young boy's) provisions at the disposal of the community, he was reminding the people of what Ched Myers has called 'the manna tradition's censure of stored wealth in the face of community need'.[1] Wealth is made or obtained in order to be distributed, not hoarded. As we have already seen, Jesus himself chose not to hoard his miraculous powers for his own gain, instead he put them at the disposal of the community. In the desert, he refused to turn the stones into bread to satisfy his own hunger. He waived the opportunity to perform a miracle

---

[1] Ched Myers, *Jesus' New Economy of Grace*.

for his own personal advantage. Faced with the crowd's hunger, however, Jesus had no hesitation in using his powers to meet their needs.

He restored the Sabbath

As with so many aspects of the Law, the Pharisees had reduced the Sabbath provisions to a legalistic set of requirements, done out of duty rather than joy and in a spirit of self-righteousness rather than humility. They had entirely missed the point, and consequently were in the ironic position of demolishing the real meaning of the Sabbath in a petty and vacuous bid to observe its outward stipulations.

Jesus cut a swathe through this empty legalism. Matthew 12 and Mark 2 record how he walked through some cornfields on a Sabbath day. Feeling hungry, his disciples picked some ears of corn and ate them, enraging the Pharisees who declared the disciples' behaviour unlawful. It would appear that the Jubilee laws on gleaning were still practised so that the poor could glean what was left around the borders of the field. However, Jesus clearly needed to rebuke the Pharisees:

> 'Haven't you read what David did when he and his companions were hungry? He entered the house of God, and he and his companions ate the consecrated bread – which was not lawful for them to do, but only for the priests. Or haven't you read in the Law that on the Sabbath the priests in the temple desecrate the day and yet are innocent? I tell you that one greater than the temple is here. If you had known what these words mean, "I desire mercy, not sacrifice," you would not have condemned the innocent. For the Son of Man is Lord of the Sabbath' (Mt. 12:3–8).

On the very same day, Jesus went on to heal a man with a shrivelled hand. When challenged again about the legality of his behaviour, he replied:

'If any of you has a sheep and it falls into a pit on the Sabbath, will
you not take hold of it and lift it out? How much more valuable is
a man than a sheep! Therefore it is lawful to do good on the
Sabbath' (Mt. 12:11,12).

Jesus knew that the Sabbath was meant to be about freedom and
restoration. It was about rest in the widest possible sense of the
word, not the narrowest. He was not a workaholic, driven to
achieve results. He, more than anyone, knew how to rest, and how
to do so in perfect assurance of God's faithfulness and provision
(cf. Lk. 8:22–25; Jn. 11:6), but he also knew that the Sabbath was
about setting people free, not binding them. In his kindness, God
made the Sabbath for man, not man for the Sabbath (cf. Mk. 2:27).
Consequently, Jesus had no qualms about doing 'good' on this day.
As well as the healing of the man with a shrivelled hand, the
Gospels record three other healings carried out by Jesus on a
Sabbath day – the healing of the crippled woman (Lk. 13), the healing of the invalid at the pool (Jn. 5) and the healing of the man born
blind (Jn. 9). In all these healings, Jesus' argument is based on the
principle that 'if a sheep, then surely a man!' If the Pharisees
showed mercy to a sheep, how much more should they to a man?
   Jesus states that mercy is at the very heart of the law, not religious observance. He quotes from the prophet Hosea: 'For I desire
mercy, not sacrifice, and acknowledgement of God rather than
burnt offerings' (Hos. 6:6). Hosea described a people who practise
religious duties but who 'practise deceit' (7:1) and 'the merchant
uses dishonest scales; he loves to defraud' (12:7). God desires merciful actions rather than ritualistic legalism. As Lord of the Sabbath,
Jesus has come to give *shabbat* rest and if that means feeding the
hungry or setting captives free on the Sabbath, so be it.

A friend of sinners

One of the activities that characterised Jesus' ministry was his
regular habit of having meals with social outcasts. He welcomed

their company (Lk. 15:2) and reclined at table with them (Mk. 2:15). This was Jesus' way of caring for the poor, the widows, fatherless and the aliens – along with the tax collectors and sinners. This was his expression of Jubilee generosity and solidarity: 'When you give a luncheon or dinner, do not invite your friends, your brothers or relatives, or your rich neighbours; if you do, they may invite you back and so you will be repaid. But when you give a banquet, invite the poor, the crippled, the lame, the blind, and you will be blessed' (Lk. 14:12–14).

Such was Jesus' habit of generous table fellowship that he became labelled as a friend (*philos*) of tax collectors and sinners (Mt. 11:19; Lk. 7:34). Jeremias had this to say about meals:

> It is important to realise that in the east, even today, to invite a man to a meal is an honour. It was an offer of peace, trust, brotherhood and forgiveness; in short, sharing a table meant sharing life . . . In Judaism in particular, table-fellowship means fellowship before God (Joachim Jeremias, *New Testament Theology*).

As such, table fellowship often acted as a tool for reinforcing social hierarchies and boundaries. Jesus therefore greatly honoured the social outcasts when he broke with social expectations and shared festive meals with them. By doing this, he also challenged the practice of separation in the Pharisees' table fellowship that they felt was a divine call to purity.

Zacchaeus and Jubilee

The story of Zacchaeus, the tax collector that everyone hated, is a prime example of someone touched by the spirit of Jubilee (Lk. 19:1–10). In his desperation to see Jesus, he climbed a tree hoping to catch a glimpse of him without being spotted. Jesus sees him up the sycamore tree, calls out to him and says he would like to be his dinner guest and stay at his house, to the anger of his disciples and the crowd. Zacchaeus responds to this unexpected and extravagant grace by saying: 'Look, Lord! Here and now I give half of my possessions to the poor, and if I have cheated anybody out of anything, I will pay back four times the amount' (Lk. 19:8). What a response to Jesus' offer of friendship. Giving half his wealth away did not mean he would live the rest of his life in poverty, but it did mean that he was no longer a prisoner to material riches. Jesus had not even preached a sermon to him about tithing or stewardship! He did not need to. By responding generously, Zacchaeus demonstrated that he had been genuinely touched by the grace of God.

When a person confessed to fraud and made voluntary restitution, the Law required him to return the amount stolen plus twenty per cent (Lev. 6:2–5; Num. 5:5–7). If a thief was caught in the act he must pay back double (Ex. 22:7). But a man stealing any essential possession was required to pay back fourfold (Ex. 22:1; 2 Sam. 12:6). Zacchaeus, fully repentant, voluntarily imposed on himself the full restitution required by the Law. This was a remarkable act. He had gone beyond the requirements of the Law because he had experienced the extravagant love of God.

Jesus responded to this generous act by saying: 'Today salvation has come to this house because this man, too, is a son of Abraham' (Lk. 19:9). In other words, Zacchaeus had been an outcast, but now he had been restored to his own people. Scholars have noticed an interesting play on words here. The Hebrew word for salvation is *yeshu'ah* and Jesus' name in Hebrew is *Yeshua*. *Yeshua*/salvation has literally 'come to this house'. That is one of the things God does to us when he saves us; he brings us into his family. Those who have been touched by God's love discover new brothers and friends in his family.

What happened to Zacchaeus is very exciting. He was touched by the spirit of Jubilee. Zacchaeus distributed his wealth with Jubilee generosity, was set free from his addiction to money, made restitution for his fraud and rediscovered family as a son of Abraham.

Cleansing of the temple

Jesus proclaimed the message of the kingdom not only in words, but also in actions. Many of his actions offended the traditionalists including his table-fellowship with tax collectors and sinners. One of his most daring acts to demonstrate the justice of the kingdom took place when he cleared the money changers and traders from the temple. When pilgrims came to worship at the temple, they had to do two things. One was to buy a sacrificial animal that had been certified as ritually clean by the priests. The best place to do this was from the traders in the temple who had a special arrangement with the priests. It was of course many times more expensive than buying it outside the temple but there would have been no guarantee that it would be acceptable. In order to buy the sacrificial animal, the pilgrims needed the correct currency. They could exchange this with the money changers in the temple for a fee of ten per cent. Secondly, the pilgrims had to pay a temple tax. This could only be done using a special temple coin since the Roman coins, which had idolatrous images on them, were unacceptable. The charge to exchange foreign currency for a temple coin was twelve per cent. Again you could do this through the money changers. People who exchanged money were also able to make loans (in fact the table over which money was passed was called a 'bank'). Further evidence of this is when, in the Parable of the Talents, Jesus suggested that the servant should have invested the money (with the money changers) to accumulate interest (Mt. 25:27).

This was an iniquitous racket. The whole practice was an unjust cartel and the poor were being fleeced. The authorities were making money out of religion. Jesus did not merely speak out against this injustice. Placing himself in the tradition of the Old Testament prophet, an outraged Jesus took a whip to chase away the animals and their vendors, overturned the tables of the money changers and caused chaos. So much for the gentle Jesus meek and mild! There is a place for righteous anger, and this was it. Through his actions he proclaimed God's kingdom and his justice. This audacious act demonstrates that there will be occasions when his disciples will have to take positive action against unjust situations even if it endangers their lives. Jubilee practitioners cannot sit passively when confronted by injustice.

Jesus' Jubilee Words

Seek first the kingdom

In a lengthy discourse, Jesus encouraged his disciples not to worry about 'what you will eat or drink; or about your body, what you will wear' (Mt. 6:25). He argued that if the birds of the air and the lilies in the fields are fed and clothed, how much more will the heavenly Father provide for his children? And besides, 'Who of you by worrying can add a single hour to his life?' (Mt. 6:27).

> 'So do not worry, saying, "What shall we eat?" or "What shall we drink?" or "What shall we wear?" For the pagans run after all these things, and your heavenly Father knows that you need them. But seek first his kingdom and his righteousness, and all these things will be given to you as well. Therefore do not worry about tomorrow, for tomorrow will worry about itself. Each day has enough trouble of its own' (Mt. 6:31–34).

The questions, 'what shall we eat or drink or wear?' are the very questions asked by the Israelites when they had the Jubilee programmes explained to them. These are Jubilee questions. 'If we have to have a year's rest, how shall we live?' they asked. In exactly the same way that God asked the Israelites to trust him then, he also asked the disciples to trust him. As we have noted, a key Jubilee principle is dependency and trust in God's provision for our needs.

The disciples' energy should instead be focused on seeking his kingdom and his righteousness. The word 'righteousness' is '*dikaiosune*' which is equally well translated as justice or social holiness. The Hebrew word '*tsedeq*' (righteousness or justice) is derived from '*tsaddiq*' meaning righteous or just. In other words, this call to seek God's righteous kingdom does not refer to personal and private holiness. As disciples of Jesus, they are to usher in his Jubilee kingdom which is characterised by justice or social holiness.

Love your neighbour

Various rabbis over the previous centuries sought to summarise the Law. In the Parable of the Good Samaritan (Lk. 10:25–37), we have one such summary: '"Love the Lord your God with all your heart and with all your soul and with all your strength and with all your mind"; and, "Love your neighbour as yourself".' This is a brilliant synthesis of Deut. 6:5 and Lev. 19:18. Mark's Gospel seems to indicate that this summary was unique to Jesus (Mk. 12:28–34). In fact, the teacher of the law having heard Jesus' summary of the law even went on to say that to love God and love your neighbour 'is more important than all burnt offerings and sacrifices' (v. 33). No wonder Jesus said: 'You are not far from the kingdom of God' (v. 34). This man had understood the true nature of the Law.

We saw that the Jubilee programmes were in fact outworkings of the command to love our neighbour. In the Old Testament, the neighbour was understood as a fellow Israelite and a member of the clan or extended family. In the New Testament, Jesus re-interprets this neighbourly love to outcasts and even their national enemies. In the story about sheep and goats (Mt. 25:31–46) the righteous 'sheep' were invited to inherit the kingdom because of their practical love.

'For I was hungry and you gave me something to eat, I was thirsty and you gave me something to drink, I was a stranger and you invited me in, I needed clothes and you clothed me, I was sick and you looked after me, I was in prison and you came to visit me.' Then the righteous will answer him, 'Lord, when did we see you hungry and feed you, or thirsty and give you something to drink? When did we see you a stranger and invite you in, or needing clothes and clothe you? When did we see you sick or in prison and go to visit you?'

The King will reply, 'I tell you the truth, whatever you did for one of the least of these brothers of mine, you did for me' (Mt. 25:35–40).

In this story, Jesus defines neighbour as the social outcasts in need of *shabbat* rest. Interestingly, Jesus described them as 'these brothers of mine'. In this he is expressing the solidarity of the Jubilee family. We should extend Jubilee blessings to the social outcasts because they too are part of the family.

In the parable of the Good Samaritan, the neighbour is the Samaritan, a national enemy of the Jews. In this well-known parable, the Samaritan showed compassion towards the unconscious man (Lk. 10:33) and extended unexpected generosity even to the extent of promising to reimburse the innkeeper for any extra expenses (v. 35). The expert in the Law who had asked Jesus the question: 'Who is my neighbour?' was forced in the end to answer that it was 'the one who had mercy on him' (v. 37). Through this parable, Jesus had defined 'neighbour' to include Israel's national enemy and as such his disciples needed to extend Jubilee generosity to them as well.

Laws on lending and debt cancellation

We saw how the Jubilee laws prohibited lending with interest to fellow Israelites and for cancellation of debts every seven years. We also saw how these laws were flouted. In the New Testament, lending with interest was part of everyday life and this was carried out by professional money lenders. We see this in the parable of the Two Debtors:

'Two men owed money to a certain money-lender. One owed him five hundred denarii, and the other fifty. Neither of them had the money to pay him back, so he cancelled the debts of both. Now which of them will love him more?' Simon replied, 'I suppose the one who had the bigger debt cancelled.' 'You have judged correctly,' Jesus said (Lk. 7:41–43).

Jesus was no ivory tower theologian expounding abstract truths. He tells this parable using a background that would be familiar to everyone. What is interesting though is his reference to the Jubilee practice of debt cancellation. Of course this is only a story but it is clear that Jesus knew about the requirement of the Law regarding debt cancellation. Secondly, this parable was told in the context of a sinful woman washing Jesus' feet with her tears in gratitude for her forgiveness and restoration (Lk. 7:36–50). Jesus commends her during the dinner party with his Pharisee host: 'Therefore, I tell you, her many sins have been forgiven – for she loved much. But he who has been forgiven little loves little' (Lk. 7:47). The word 'forgive' is again the word *'aphesis'* for release or cancellation of debt.

On lending itself, Jesus had some challenging things to say too:

'And if you lend to those from whom you expect repayment, what credit is that to you? Even "sinners" lend to "sinners", expecting to be repaid in full. But love your enemies, do good to them, and lend to them without expecting to get anything back. Then your reward will be great, and you will be sons of the Most High, because he is kind to the ungrateful and wicked. Be merciful, just as your Father is merciful' (Lk. 6:34–36).

Clearly Jesus does not approve of private loans with interest. His instruction, however, to 'lend without expecting anything back' sounds distinctly like going beyond Jubilee debt cancellation. Jesus is instructing his disciples not to lend at all, but to give.

With lending, even without interest, the lender gets his capital back. With giving, nothing comes back. In the New Testament, Jesus teaches giving rather than lending or tithing. 'Give to everyone who asks you, and if anyone takes what belongs to you [a euphemism for stealing?], do not demand it back' (Lk. 6:30) and again, 'Give to the one who asks you, and do not turn away from the one who wants to borrow from you' (Mt. 5:42). Secondly, Jesus gives these instructions in the context of enemy-loving. He wants his disciples to give money to their enemies when they are in need! I think it would have been a difficult enough task to persuade the disciples to lend money to their friends, never mind giving to them. But to imagine that they would give money to help their enemies was surely too much to ask. And yet here it is. This is how radical his disciples have to be in relation to caring for the poor. We have already seen the group of women who gave money to support the travelling band of disciples. But in the Old Testament, we have no examples of enemy-loving of this nature. The giving, lending, debt cancellation and wealth distribution were confined to fellow Israelites. Jesus radically extends Jubilee generosity to the enemy.

Parables and sayings about money

In Old Testament times, wealth was measured by the land owned, number of animals and crops. In a simple agricultural society there was little need for money. By New Testament times, the economy had changed. The majority of the people were landless and worked as servants or day labourers and were paid with money. Money became the measure of one's wealth. It is not surprising therefore that Jesus had so much to say about money.

Jesus had a stern warning for those who pursued wealth for personal gain and overlooked the needs of others. The parable of the Rich Man and Lazarus (Lk. 16:19–31) tells the story of a man who lived in luxury every day whilst a beggar named Lazarus lay by his gate longing to eat the crumbs that fell from the rich man's table. When both men died, the rich man went to *Hades* and Lazarus went to Abraham's bosom. The rich man calls up from hell to Abraham, asking him to have pity on him and to send Lazarus to dip the tip of his finger in water to cool his tongue. His request is refused. It is too late. His lack of generosity in his own lifetime has led to this impasse:

> Abraham replied, 'Son, remember that in your lifetime you received your good things, while Lazarus received bad things, but now he is comforted here and you are in agony. And besides all this, between us and you a great chasm has been fixed, so that those who want to go from here to you cannot, nor can anyone cross over from there to us' (Lk. 16:25,26).

The rich man had selfishly used his wealth. He had enjoyed *more than he needed* whilst another, within reach of his help, suffered because he had *less than he needed*. It contrasts sharply with the story of the feeding of the 5,000. In both cases there is a reaping, but the nature of the reaping is very different. The young boy's willingness to share his loaves and fishes reaped a blessing – the multiplication of his gift – whereas in the parable the rich man's greed reaps judgement – eternal separation from God. The beggar, meanwhile, finds rest and vindication, for God is the champion of the poor and oppressed.

It is a parable that has deliberate shock value. The vocabulary of Abraham's reply is carefully chosen to emphasise the finality of the rich man's fate, and its awful contrast with that of Lazarus. Jesus wanted his disciples to be under no illusions. It was impossible to enjoy a relationship with God and simultaneously store up wealth in blatant disregard of another's need. So important was this message that he returned to it again and again:

> 'Do not store up for yourselves treasures on earth, where moth and rust destroy, and where thieves break in and steal. But store

up for yourselves treasure in heaven, where moth and rust do not destroy, and where thieves do not break in and steal. For where your treasure is, there your heart will be also . . . No one can serve two masters. Either he will hate the one and love the other, or he will be devoted to the one and despise the other. You cannot serve both God and Money' (Mt. 6:19–21, 24; see also Lk. 12:13–21).

Just as the manna rotted if it was held over for another day (see Ex. 16:20), so worldly treasures would decay if stored up. Such hoarding behaviour was inconsistent with trust in God. It was simply not possible to behave like that and be fully devoted to him. It should perhaps come as no surprise then that Jesus personified money here as a sort of god. Nonetheless it has some fairly startling implications. As Jacques Ellul has said, Jesus' choice of words 'reveals something exceptional about money, for Jesus did not usually use deifications and personifications. What Jesus is revealing is that money is a power.'[2]

Since money was capable of rivalling God in terms of loyalty and worship, Jesus' disciples really needed to be free from its control. Some of the people that Jesus met accepted this, and others did not. Zacchaeus fell into the first category, the rich young ruler fell into the second:

'Look, Lord! Here and now I give half of my possessions to the poor, and if I have cheated anybody out of anything, I will pay back four times the amount.' Jesus said to him, 'Today salvation has come to this house, because this man, too, is a son of Abraham' (Lk. 19:8,9).

'You still lack one thing. Sell everything you have and give to the poor, and you will have treasure in heaven. Then come, follow me.' When he heard this, he became very sad, because he was a man of great wealth. Jesus looked at him and said, 'How hard it is for the

---

[2] Jacques Ellul, *Money and Power*.

rich to enter the kingdom of God! Indeed, it is easier for a camel to go through the eye of a needle than for a rich man to enter the kingdom of God' (Lk. 18:22–25).

Giving alms or charity was encouraged and was something that every righteous Jew did as part of their religious observance. The rich young ruler, however, would have been stunned by Jesus' advice to sell everything he had and give to the poor. He would have understood advice to increase his giving to charity but to sell everything for the poor in order to follow Jesus would have been an act of outrageous generosity or madness. That Jesus had counselled him in this manner suggests how this young ruler was captive or addicted to his wealth. Whilst this was the only recorded occasion when Jesus asked someone to sell *everything* he had, he nevertheless expected his disciples to give away part of their possessions to the poor.

'Do not be afraid, little flock, for your Father has been pleased to give you the kingdom. Sell your possessions and give to the poor. Provide purses for yourselves that will not wear out, a treasure in heaven that will not be exhausted, where no thief comes near and no moth destroys. For where your treasure is, there your heart will be also' (Lk. 12:32–34).

Selling of possessions and giving to the poor was part of the discipleship requirements of this new rabbi. This is the Jubilee distribution of wealth and expression of social holiness and generosity. Jesus' only caution was that these acts of mercy (giving) should not be done in order to draw the praises of people (Mt. 6:1–4). He also taught that such acts of generosity were better than ritual purity (Lk.11:41).

Richard Foster[3] makes an interesting point about the challenges that Jesus laid before these two individuals:

---

[3] Richard Foster, *Money, Sex and Power*.

Do you see what an utter contrast this is to the normal means of evangelism today? Our method is to get them 'saved' and then later on instruct them in 'Christian stewardship.' For us, salvation usually consists in assenting to three or four statements and saying the prescribed prayer. But Jesus warns people to count the cost of discipleship before they ever enter into it . . . For Christ, money is an idolatry we must be converted *from* in order to be converted *to* him. The rejection of the god mammon is a necessary precondition to becoming a disciple of Jesus.

It is no wonder that Jesus commended the widow who put 'all she had to live on' in the temple treasury (Lk. 21:4). It may have only been two small coins, but her gift (unlike those given by the rich) signified total commitment. She recognised and accepted her utter dependence on God.

Not so the teachers of the Law who devoured the houses of such widows (Lk. 20:47). These men were guilty of using God and oppressing their neighbours. They had an outward veneer of righteousness – reciting prayers, teaching the Law – but their hearts were rotten. It was this kind of hypocrisy and hollowness that Jesus consistently condemned:

> Woe to you teachers of the law and Pharisees, you hypocrites! You give a tenth of your spices – mint, dill and cumin. But you have neglected the more important matters of the law – justice [*krisis*], mercy [*eleos*] and faithfulness [*pistin*]. You should have practised the latter, without neglecting the former. You blind guides! You strain out a gnat but swallow a camel (Mt. 23:23,24).

Just as Jesus exposed the empty legalism of the Pharisees' approach to the Sabbath, so here he was exposing the empty legalism of their approach to tithing. He was not saying that tithing does not matter, but that it is not enough. If it is not the outward expression of an inner devotion to God and a commitment to love one's neighbour, then its value is lost. The letter of the law was never meant to replace the spirit of the law.

The Sermon on the Mount

The Sermon on the Mount contains some of Jesus' most powerful teaching to his disciples about the radical behaviour and attitudes as subjects of the 'kingdom of heaven'. As Moses gave the Law at Mount Sinai, so here Jesus gives his Sermon on the Mount. And Jesus takes up many of the issues in the Law of Moses except that he radically interprets them. A regular refrain is 'You have heard that it was said (i.e. by Moses), but I tell you . . .' Over the course of this sermon, found in chapters 5, 6 and 7 of Matthew (and partly recorded also in chapter 6 of Luke), Jesus described the revolutionary values and attitudes that operate in the Jubilee kingdom. Jesus taught his disciples to go beyond what is required under the Law of Moses. He came not to abolish the Law but to fulfil it (Mt. 5:17), interpreting it both in a deeper way as well as setting a higher standard. Murder is now defined as hating someone in your heart (Mt. 5:21,22), adultery is looking at a woman lustfully (Mt. 5:27,28). Proportionate retaliation ('an eye for an eye, a tooth for a tooth') is to give way to turning the other cheek and going the second mile: 'If someone strikes you on the right cheek, turn to him the other also. And if someone wants to sue you and take your tunic, let him have your cloak as well. If someone forces you to go one mile, go with him two miles' (Mt. 5:39–41).

Jesus is calling for a higher level of social behaviour among his disciples than that required under the Law. 'For I tell you that unless your righteousness [*dikaiousune*] surpasses that of the Pharisees and the teachers of the law, you will certainly not enter the kingdom of heaven' (Mt. 5:20). Nowhere is this higher standard more demanding and radical than the call to enemy-loving. 'You have heard that it was said, "Love your neighbour and hate your enemy." But I tell you: Love your enemies and pray for those who persecute you' (Mt. 5:43,44). Jesus' argument was that even sinners and tax collectors can show love to those who love them but the disciples had to 'be perfect, therefore, as your heavenly Father is perfect' (Mt. 5:48). This saying is based on Deut. 18:13 'be blameless' (Greek *teleios*, Hebrew *tamim*) and Leviticus 19:2 'Be holy because I . . . am holy.' In the Old Testament times the people were to be holy in order that God might dwell among them (Lev. 26:11) so now the disciples were to be holy because Jesus, the Word become flesh, was dwelling with them (Jn. 1:14). In the corresponding passage in Luke, the disciples are called to 'be merciful, just as your Father is merciful'. The word 'merciful' is the Greek *'oiktirmon'* and is better translated as 'compassionate' and has the idea of pity or sympathy shown to the unfortunate and needy. Within the context of Jesus' teachings about lending money to their enemies, it could even be paraphrased as 'be generous, just as your Father is generous' (Lk. 6:36). To lend to one's enemies without expecting to get anything back is truly an expression of Jubilee generosity.

In the Beatitudes, we see the 'beautiful attitudes' required of the disciples in the community and hear further echoes of Jubilee:

> Blessed are you who are poor,
>   for yours is the kingdom of God.
> Blessed are you who hunger now,
>   for you will be satisfied.
> Blessed are you who weep now,
>   for you will laugh.
> Blessed are you when men hate you,
>   when they exclude you and insult you
>   and reject your name as evil,
>   because of the Son of Man (Lk. 6:20–22).

Jeremias points out that Semitic languages often omit the qualifying word *'only'*, even when the sentence requires it. He argues that this is the case here and therefore 'the first beatitude means that salvation is destined *only* for beggars and sinners.' The reign of God belongs *to the poor alone.*

Matthew's version of the Beatitudes adds a spiritual dimension to this and blesses those who are poor *in spirit* and hunger and thirst *for righteousness* (Mt. 5:3–10). Furthermore those who show mercy and are pure in heart are also blessed and the makers of *shalom* shall be called sons of God. The poor (*ptochoi*) in spirit includes those who are humbled by their long economic and social distress and as such have confidence only in God. The good news Jesus brings is only for the poor – economically and spiritually.

The Lord's Prayer

'Our Father in heaven,
hallowed be your name,
your kingdom come,
your will be done
on earth as it is in heaven.
Give us today our daily bread.
Forgive us our debts,
as we also have forgiven our debtors.
And lead us not into temptation,
but deliver us from the evil one' (Mt. 6:9–13).

As Jeremias notes, 'The parables of the two debtors (Lk. 7:41–43), the unmerciful servant (Matt. 18:23–25) and the love of the father (Luke 15:11–32) show that in the good news what happens is the remission of debts.'[4]

The word 'forgive' is *'aphesis'* which means 'to release or cancel' and the word 'debt' is *'opheilema'* which means literal 'debt'. The Aramiac word *'hoba'* (debt) from which the Greek *'opheilema'*

---

[4] Joachim Jeremias, *New Testament Theology.*

would have derived, was often also used for 'sin' and 'transgression'. This is a Jubilee prayer asking God to help his disciples with debt cancellation. Jesus' use of the word for 'debt' may have been deliberate to create ambiguity so that both monetary and spiritual debts may be included. That this included moral sin is clear with a later statement: 'For if you forgive men when they sin (*paraptoma*) against you, your heavenly Father will also forgive you' (Mt. 6:14). The one who prays for God's cancellation of debt should be prepared also to cancel the debts others owe them. Within the family of believers, the disciples should be willing to forgive each others' debts – monetary as well as wrongdoings.

The Lord's Prayer reminds us that trusting God is the basis of Jubilee living. It also teaches us that debt cancellation has become a continuous duty – through the ready offer of forgiveness to those who sin against us. This is a tough requirement, but necessary if we are to enjoy a relationship with each other and the Father (see the parable of the Unmerciful Servant, Mt. 18:21–35). By cancelling our debts, Jesus has enabled us to return to the Father. If we fail to cancel the debts of others, we jeopardise this restoration. The restoration of family relationships was an important aspect of the Jubilee, but Jesus has redefined family as the body of believers in restored communion with each other and their heavenly Father.

The kingdom of heaven

Jesus portrayed the kingdom not as some distant place or time but rather as an immanent reality in the lives of his disciples. This is true, but it is an incomplete picture. Through his death on the cross, Jesus caused the power of the kingdom of heaven to break through into the world. He was proclaiming a Jubilee – cancelling debts, setting slaves free, restoring relationships. But it was an ongoing Jubilee, one that continues to this day. Through Jesus, we are to act as conduits of his ongoing Jubilee blessings and thereby continue the process of kingdom building until the work is finished.

It is not until this Jubilee has ended that the kingdom will be fully established. At that time, the final Jubilee act will occur – the land will be redeemed once and for all and restored to its rightful owner: 'Then I saw a new heaven and a new earth, for the first heaven and the first earth had passed away, and there was no longer any sea. I saw the Holy City, the new Jerusalem, coming down out of heaven from God, prepared as a bride beautifully dressed for her husband' (Rev. 21:1,2).

In this microcosm of a holy nation, the Jesus community expressed a radical new lifestyle. They had all things in common, sharing a common purse and trusted God to provide for their needs. Social holiness was evident among them and the poor and social outcasts seemed to be attracted to them. They had a higher standard of behaviour, living 'beyond' the Law. They had the sense of an extended family at peace with themselves and one another. *Shalom* and *shabbat* rest were experienced and their mission was to share this good news with everyone as they travelled around Israel.

What Jesus was doing by his words and deeds was radically reinterpreting the Jubilee, making it an everyday duty in the lives of his disciples rather than an event that took place every fifty years. And this condition of perpetual Jubilee had a new name: 'the kingdom of heaven'. This kingdom was not some distant place or time; it was the immanent, ongoing rule of God, inaugurated through Jesus and continued through the lives of his followers, expressed in the fruit of Jubilee actions and attitudes.

What we see in the Gospels is only the beginning of a fresh attempt by Jesus and his disciples to work out Jubilee principles in a new era of changed economics and politics. The full expression of this will only become evident in the Acts of the Apostles, to which we now turn.

6

Jubilee in Acts

We began this book looking at Jesus' Jubilee manifesto, which Luke highlighted in chapter 4 of his Gospel. From there we've tried to portray something of the comprehensive vision of the Jubilee programmes – which ultimately has meant trying to capture something of the comprehensiveness of God's love and care for his people and his creation. In the last chapter, we looked at aspects of Jesus' ministry in which his practices of Jubilee are perhaps most explicit. But Jesus died and then rose again. How, if at all, does his resurrection affect our understanding of Jubilee and how it is to be worked out?

Jesus is an example of what we should do in working out Jubilee. We should look for dynamic equivalents for what Jesus was doing amongst Israel and then do likewise in the world in which we live. But it would be a mistake to think that Jesus' life was *simply* an example to be followed. I suggest that two aspects of Jesus' work are of particular relevance for understanding of our topic of the Jubilee today. Firstly, that in his ascension and giving of the Spirit, Jesus was finally restoring Israel, not in a nationalistic way, but in such a way that it was now compelled by the Spirit to go beyond its own boundaries and into the world with Jubilee hope. Secondly, that in his death and resurrection, Jesus conquered every principality and power (what is often referred to as a *Christus Victor* view on the atonement) and that, for today, this victory is effective over the power of consumerism

– which has been described as the spirit of the age, and surely also one of the greatest powers to keep us from being a Jubilee people. These two aspects of Jesus' work are inseparable. Just as the year of Jubilee was announced on the Day of Atonement, so also Jesus in his death-resurrection-giving of the Spirit effected a new era of Jubilee, to which we now turn.

Pentecost and Sinai

On the eve of his crucifixion, Jesus reassured his disciples that when the time came for him to return to the Father, the Holy Spirit would come in his place: 'I will ask the Father, and he will give you another Counsellor to be with you for ever – the Spirit of truth' (Jn. 14:16,17). After his resurrection, before ascending into heaven, he renewed his pledge: 'Do not leave Jerusalem, but wait for the gift my Father promised, which you have heard me speak about. For John baptised with water, but in a few days you will be baptised with the Holy Spirit' (Acts 1:4,5).

Why was this gift so important? Why couldn't the disciples begin their missionary activities straightaway? Jesus gave them this reason: 'you will receive power when the Holy Spirit comes on you; and you will be my witnesses in Jerusalem, and in all Judea and Samaria, and to the ends of the earth' (Acts 1:8).

If Jesus needed the anointing of the Spirit to fulfil his Jubilee mission (Lk. 4:18), how much more his disciples?

Forty days after his resurrection, Jesus ascended into heaven. His disciples returned to Jerusalem to await the gift that he had promised them. On the day of Pentecost, they were all gathered together in one place.

> Suddenly a sound like the blowing of a violent wind came from heaven and filled the whole house where they were sitting. They saw what seemed to be tongues of fire that separated and came to rest on each of them. All of them were filled with the Holy Spirit

and began to speak in other tongues as the Spirit enabled them
(Acts 2:2–4).

This is a passage that is familiar to all Christians. A common
way of understanding the birth of the early church on the day
of Pentecost (Acts 2–4) is from the perspective of the prophecies
of Joel. After all, Peter himself quoted Joel to explain the phe-
nomenon of the rushing wind, the fire, and the speaking in
tongues:

> 'This is what was spoken by the prophet Joel:
> "In the last days, God says,
> I will pour out my Spirit on all people.
> Your sons and daughters will prophesy,
> your young men will see visions,
> your old men will dream dreams.
> Even on my servants, both men and women,
> I will pour out my Spirit in those days,
> and they will prophesy"' (Acts 2:16–18).

Seen from the perspective of the prophet Joel, the emphases of
charismatic interpretations of the giving of the Spirit at
Pentecost have inevitably focused on the supernatural phenom-
ena of the day. Understanding Pentecost in this one way only,
however, is like trying to take in the whole perspective of a high
mountain from the vantage of a small hill. Yes we will see something of what is on the mountain, but we will not be able to see
it all.

We argue that the wider perspective from which to understand
Pentecost is in fact the giving of the Law at Sinai, and of the
nation being restored under a new law of the Spirit (Acts 1:6).
This can be argued for a number of reasons. First, to this day the
Jews celebrate Pentecost as the anniversary of the giving of the
Law at Sinai. In post-exilic Judaism, Pentecost was celebrated as

the anniversary of the giving of the Law and confirmation of the covenant at Sinai. Our earliest authorities for identifying Pentecost with the anniversary of the Law-giving is the book of Jubilees, according to which the same day is the anniversary of the covenant with Noah. Second, just as the Law was given at Sinai to form the new nation of Israel, so now the Spirit is given to form a new people, the church – 'a chosen people, a royal priesthood, a holy nation, a people belonging to God' (1 Pet. 2:9). And just as Israel was to be distinctive in its nationhood, so likewise should the church be as a holy nation, in part characterised by Jubilee generosity.

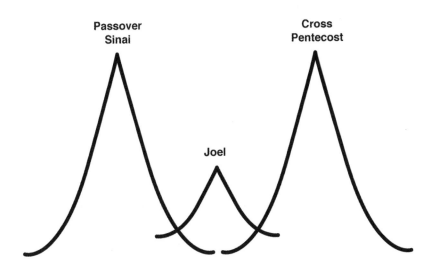

Fifty days after the original Passover, Moses ascended up Mount Sinai where he received from God the Law carved on tablets of stone, then brought it down to the people. And now, fifty days after the new Passover, Jesus the Passover Lamb (1 Cor. 5:7), ascended to be with the Father and sent down his promised

Spirit, to bring the law that is 'written on human hearts' (2 Cor. 3:3–6).[1]

The Jubilee Significance of Pentecost

Viewed from the perspective of Sinai, the most miraculous thing about Pentecost was not the spiritual manifestation. It was the practice of Jubilee by this new nation expressed in its economic sharing.

> They devoted themselves to the apostles' teaching and to the fellowship, to the breaking of bread and to prayer. Everyone was filled with awe, and many wonders and miraculous signs were done by the apostles. All the believers were together and had everything in common. Selling their possessions and goods, they gave to anyone as he had need. Every day they continued to meet together in the temple courts. They broke bread in their homes and ate together with glad and sincere hearts, praising God and enjoying the favour of all the people. And the Lord added to their number daily those who were being saved (Acts 2:42–47).

This was Jubilee love in action. The new believers, full of the Spirit, began to sell their possessions and goods that were surplus to their needs and shared the proceeds with the other believers in need. Something extraordinary was happening here. We need to be reminded that these are hard-nosed Jews from the

---

[1] Luke deliberately shows that many of the sights and sounds that had accompanied the giving of the Law at Mount Sinai were echoed in the account of the giving of the Spirit at Pentecost. Compare Exodus 20:18 with Acts 2:1–4. The very word Pentecost – meaning 'fiftieth', because it fell on the fiftieth day after the Passover – further confirms the correlation. Furthermore, the coming of the Spirit was accompanied by a loud sound from heaven reminiscent of the thunder and shakings at Sinai.

Diaspora expressing extraordinary generosity to fellow Jewish pilgrims who were complete strangers. They had all things in common and apart from meeting daily in the temple courts for prayer and fellowship, they were in and out of each other's homes every day, breaking bread together. This does not mean they were having a formal 'eucharist' or 'communion' daily. Breaking bread meant having meals together. What is happening here? I believe the Holy Spirit was leading the early church in its expression of Jubilee and re-discovering 'family'. They were strangers when they arrived in Jerusalem as pilgrims, but when the Spirit came, they discovered that they, in the Messiah Jesus, were brothers and sisters belonging to the same family. Hence the acts of generosity expressed through their economic sharing and daily caring for each other. This also answers an earlier question: why wasn't the Jubilee practised in the Old Testament? The answer is that the requirements of Jubilee were so tough that it could only happen through the generous outpouring of the Spirit. Jubilee was impossible in human strength alone which was why the Israelites failed in the Old Testament. It was only possible through the supernatural love that results from the coming of the Spirit. And that was why the disciples had to wait in Jerusalem for the coming of the Spirit, without whom the Jubilee gospel of good news to the poor would not have been possible.

There were two pillars that characterised the church at Pentecost: believing and belonging. The people 'believed' when they heard the preaching of the word and 'belonged' when they were added to their new family. This need for belonging has not diminished today. When visiting an old folks home in the West and seeing all the lonely people, Mother Teresa commented that whilst the developing countries suffered from an epidemic of poverty, the West was suffering from an epidemic of loneliness.

The Holy Spirit was causing economic upheaval in the lives of the new believers. No formal Jubilee had been proclaimed, the

Law did not impose this redistribution of wealth, rather it was all initiated and led by the Spirit. What's more, these acts of generosity seemed to have evangelistic power. The number of disciples was increasing. Doubtless this was in part due to the authority of the apostles' preaching, but it also appears to have been attributable to their radical lifestyle:

> All the believers were one in heart and mind. No-one claimed that any of his possessions was his own, but they shared everything they had. With great power the apostles continued to testify to the resurrection of the Lord Jesus, and much grace was upon them all. There were no needy persons among them. For from time to time those who owned lands or houses sold them, brought the money from the sales and put it at the apostles' feet, and it was distributed to anyone as he had need.
>
> Joseph, a Levite from Cyprus, whom the apostles called Barnabas (which means Son of Encouragement), sold a field he owned and brought the money and put it at the apostles' feet (Acts 4:32–37).

Sandwiched in the middle of two sentences about the disciples' economic lifestyle is a sentence about the success of their evangelistic efforts (Acts 4:33). The implication is clear. We cannot separate our verbal proclamation from our practical witness. Jubilee living has evangelistic power (cf. Jn. 13:35). The disciples' lifestyle showed an integrity of character and purpose that was immensely attractive.

What is really startling from this passage are the words: 'There were no needy [literally 'poor'] persons among them.' This is the fulfilment of the Jubilee promise from Deut. 15:4,5: 'there should be no poor among you . . . if only you fully obey the LORD your God and are careful to follow all these [Jubilee] commands I am giving you today'. As we have seen, Israel did not implement the Jubilee programmes resulting in the predictable rise in socio-economic injustice over time. But now, over 1,500 years later, through the coming of the Spirit, the Jubilee promise that 'there will be no poor among you' is finally fulfilled amongst this new community of believers. How appropriate that it should be fulfilled in Jerusalem, from where the commencement of the Jubilee was meant to be announced through the blowing of the *shofar* from the temple courts. And just so we understand the scale of what was happening, Luke informs us that there were about 5,000 men, excluding women and children, in the church by this stage (Acts 4:4). Even with such large numbers, he observed that there were no poor among them. Quite remarkable given the socio-economic conditions of the first century. How many churches or communities can make that claim?

This new community of goods and economic sharing should not be interpreted as some experiment in communism as Karl Marx would have liked. Private property was not abolished. We have seen earlier that Jubilee in the Old Testament was based on ownership of private property. It was no different here. Believers were still living in their own houses where an extraordinary amount of hospitality was taking place – 'eating and drinking' on a daily basis so that the needy were not neglected. It was not wrong to own something, and it was not compulsory to sell something. It was not wrong to be rich (cf. 1 Tim. 6:17–19). The point was that 'no-one claimed that any of his possessions was his own' (Acts 4:32). Assets were at the disposal not only of their owner but also of the wider community. Their value lay in their availability. The disciples had a renewed and redeemed vision of stewardship.

There is something else of significance in this passage from Acts 4. Words such as 'from time to time' and 'anyone as he had need' indicate a spontaneity and flexibility that had never existed under the Old Covenant. Under the Law, a Jubilee was to have been announced every fifty years. It was a remedial measure, preventing economic injustices from reaching crisis proportions. On the day of Pentecost, however, a new economic dynamic was established that would occur 'from time to time' to address the needs of the believers. Instead of a legalistic cycle of fifty years imposed on all citizens, the Jubilee expression at Pentecost was spontaneous, flexible, voluntary and could be carried out at any time as needs arose.

That the economic sharing was entirely voluntary is best illustrated by two stories. The first is the mention of Barnabas, a new Jewish believer from Cyprus who felt so moved by the needs of his new 'family' that he sold a field he owned and distributed its proceeds. The other is the tragic story of Ananias and Sapphira in Acts 5. This married couple sold a piece of property and gave only a proportion of the money to the apostles whilst claiming it was the full amount. Peter challenged them both about their deception, accusing them of lying to the Holy Spirit. He made it clear that they were under no compulsion to sell their property. They could have held on to it. Their sin was their dishonesty. Although God's judgement on sin is often delayed, it came immediately in their case – they both fell down dead. Perhaps theirs was to be a salutary lesson to the early church as it embarked upon its mission to the world. A similar fate had befallen Achan as the Israelites embarked on their conquest of the Promised Land (cf. Josh. 6 and 7).

Thankfully, the behaviour of Ananias and Sapphira was the exception rather than the rule. The majority of believers were experiencing a freedom and joy in giving that testified to the Spirit's authority in their lives. In his book *God's Young Church*, William Barclay paints a compelling picture of what life was like in this early church:

> It was a *sharing Church*. Those who were rich shared all they had with those who were poor. People in those days felt that they just could not possess too much whilst others possessed too little. In the early Church they had a very lovely custom. Every Sunday

they had what they called the Love Feast. To that feast everyone brought something, just as he was able. They pooled everything that was brought and then they sat down to share it out together. At this feast all kinds of people were sitting together. Many of the early Christians were very poor; some of them were slaves. A slave's rations in Greece were a quart of meal a day with a few figs and olives and a little wine vinegar. Very often this common meal on the Lord's Day was the only decent meal the slave got all week, and he only got it because in that early Church everyone shared with everyone else everything he had. If the spirit of Christ is really in us we will not be able to be happy if we see someone else in need and do not help him.

Under the terms of the Old Covenant, the year of Jubilee had been an event to be experienced once in a lifetime, maybe twice if you lived long enough. During his time of ministry on earth, Jesus had redefined Jubilee as an everyday duty in the lives of his followers. But this duty was to spring from willing conviction not grudging compulsion. The disciples needed their own Jubilee – to be set free from the constraints of the Law – if they were to be Jubilee practitioners themselves. The Spirit came at Pentecost to perform this act of liberation and to enable the disciples to live lives of ongoing Jubilee freedom.

Feeding the Widows and Julian the Apostate

One distinctive of the early church in Jerusalem was the daily distribution of food to the needy, especially the widows (Acts 6:1–7). Its rapid growth saw an increasing rank of poor converts joining the church. The church's response was to organise a mass feeding programme funded by the Jubilee generosity of its wealthier members. This became a distinctive practice of the New Testament church as evidenced by the instructions of Paul to Timothy (1 Tim. 5).

A good place to help us understand the crucial importance of this great tradition of caring for the poor, widows and vulnerable is the story of Julian the Apostate. Julian became the Roman Emperor in AD 361 after the death of Constantius, the successor to Constantine the Great (d.337). During his youth he was tutored by a Neo-Platonist and secretly converted from Christianity to paganism. He revealed his conversion after he ascended to the throne – hence the Apostate label. He set about trying to revive the polytheistic religion of Rome, often performing animal sacrifices in public himself. Julian hated Christianity and set about trying to stamp it out, but by non-violent means because he saw how it flourished under martyrdom. Julian discriminated against Christians in the civil service, barred them from the teaching profession, closed major cathedrals and stripped Christianity of its imperial support. He reopened temples, restored cultic worship, re-introduced the animal sacrifices to Roman gods, called himself Pontifex Maximus. But despite all his efforts, Julian could not revive the old pagan religion of the Romans.

Julian blamed the failure of his project on the Christians and their charitable work: 'These wretched Galileans feed not only their own poor, but ours as well'[2] was what he wrote to his high priests. He believed that much of Christianity's appeal grew out of its humanitarian activities – Jubilee in other words. Paganism was just not competitive against Christian acts of mercy and generosity.

The Roman Empire was a multicultural society whose provinces shared little in the way of culture. This swiftly-established empire consisted of different races, spoke different languages and practised different religions. The imperial government required nothing from these citizens except their taxes plus of course obedience.

---

[2] Rodney Stark, *The Rise of Christianity: How the Obscure, Marginal Jesus Movement became the Dominant Religious Force in the Western World in a Few Centuries.*

The problem for Julian in this kind of multicultural empire was that 'pagan hospitality' only extended to one's own kind. Charity began and ended with one's own group in society, whether it was a national or religious group. Pagans would never have fed the Christian poor. Against this backdrop, the Christian practice of 'universal charity' was surprising and attractive. Christians were feeding both their own poor and the pagan poor as well.

Julian therefore ordered his pagan hierarchy to imitate Christian charity. In a multicultural empire, where people only cared for their own kind, he tried to institute an imperial welfare system for the purpose of imitating the hated Christians. Julian believed that once an imperial system for feeding and housing the poor had been established, the Christian church would die out. It was a clever idea but Julian died in battle some nine months after he gave orders to create the Roman welfare system, so we would never know how well the system would have worked.

Julian the Apostate had made an astute and chilling observation. He believed that if the state could provide the social welfare, Christianity would die. He attributed the rapid growth of the church within the Roman Empire to its Jubilee generosity. If Julian was correct in his analysis, countries today with the most comprehensive welfare system would see a correspondingly weak church and lack of charitable activities. This has indeed been borne out by a number of studies including Anthony Gill's 'State Welfare Spending and Religiosity' (2004). He demonstrated a strong negative relationship between the level of state welfare and religiosity.

In 1889, Otto von Bismark created the world's first social security retirement system in Germany. This was followed by Franklin Roosevelt's New Deal in 1931, created during the depression in the USA, and William Beveridge's and Ernest Bevin's Welfare State – Social Security System created in 1946 in Great Britain. When President Roosevelt introduced the New

Deal, he did not believe that it would discourage the charitable and mutual-aid societies that had been caring for the poor. But Julian knew better. Christianity itself did not die out, as Julian had hoped, but much of its charitable work did. Likewise, private welfare organizations and societies shrank to a small fraction of their former size once the New Deal went into effect. They have remained so to this day.[3]

We see from this chapter how central the whole issue of caring for the poor was and is to the church's identity, growth and well-being. The Spirit-filled church of Pentecost displayed extraordinary Jubilee generosity and cared for its needy members. Discrimination was not present in any form – racial, sexual or economic – and people belonged and behaved as a family. There was social holiness as a result of their Jubilee generosity and there were no poor among them. All Spirit-filled churches should surely have these characteristics. It is worth re-quoting Lesslie Newbigin's comment on what Jesus left behind: 'It is surely a fact of inexhaustible significance that what our Lord left behind him was not a book, nor a creed, nor system of thought, nor a rule of life, but a visible community.'

Would the world continue to witness the expansion and replication of this Jubilee community? Would the church continue to proclaim a Jubilee gospel by word and deed?

---

[3] Michael Bernstein, 'The Oldest New Deal', The Yale Free Press website, http://www.yale.edu/yfp/archives/00_4_julian.html

7

From Martyrdom to Christendom

Was the new expression of Jubilee restricted to the church of the first century? Fortunately we have abundant evidence that the church continued in various ways and degrees to live as Jubilee communities right up to the fourth century. The letter of Diognetus, thought to date from the second century, described the early Christians thus:

> They dwell in their own countries, but simply as sojourners. As citizens, they share in all things with others, and yet endure all things as if foreigners. Every foreign land is to them as their native country, and every land of their birth as a land of strangers. They marry, as do all [others]; they beget children; but they do not destroy their offspring. They have a common table, but not a common bed. They are in the flesh, but they do not live after the flesh. They pass their days on earth, but they are citizens of heaven. They obey the prescribed laws, and at the same time surpass the laws by their lives. They love all men, and are persecuted by all. They are unknown and condemned; they are put to death, and restored to life. They are poor, yet make many rich; they are in lack of all things, and yet abound in all (Mathetes, 'Epistle to Diognetus', Chapter V, in Schaff, Philip, ANF01. The Apostolic Fathers with Justin Martyr and Irenaeus, http://www.ccel.org/ccel/schaff/anf01.iii.ii.v.html).

We see from this that the believers even in the second century were living a pretty radical lifestyle, one that made them stand out from the crowd. The Spirit's presence in their lives was evident, enabling them to go 'beyond' the requirements of the law in their attitude and behaviour. They were citizens of another kingdom, and yet that did not stop them from immersing themselves in the needs of the world around them. Following in the footsteps of Jesus, theirs was a wonderfully incarnational faith.

Their approach to material goods was rooted in the principles of simplicity, solidarity and Jubilee generosity – 'They offer a shared table, but not a shared bed'. Tertullian, writing at around the same period, expressed it similarly: 'We who are united in mind and soul have no hesitation about sharing property. All things are common among us except our women [i.e. wives].'[1] The boundaries they established between themselves and their neighbours were necessitated by purity, not greed.

Community of Goods

Here, then, were Christians set free by the Spirit to share and give radically in order to support the poorer members of the body, the orphans, the widows, the prisoners and even non-Christians. Tithing was seen as insufficient. It had been a requirement of the Old Covenant, and had been superseded. The coming of the Spirit had inspired Jubilee generosity or *koinonia*, a far more 'glorious' dynamic (cf. 2 Cor. 3:7–11), because it sprung from the bonds of love not the constraints of law:

> And instead of the tithes which the law commanded, the Lord said
> to divide everything we have with the poor. And he said to love
> not only our neighbours but also our enemies, and to be givers
> and sharers not only with the good but also to be liberal givers

---

[1] *Apology XXXIX*, 11.

towards those who take away our possessions (Irenaeus, circa AD 200, *Against Heresies IV*, xiv.3).

Those who came to church would bring money as well as food – oil, cheese, olives, bread, wine – as their offering. The poor brought water for diluting the communion wine. By the third century, clothes and shoes were also mentioned. These offerings would be placed on a table by the entrance and distributed by the deacons to the needy, including any absent from the meeting for various reasons. Remember that the majority of believers in the first two centuries would have been poor slaves. Even among them, we see expressions of Jubilee generosity and distribution of wealth.

It isn't clear how extensively the community of goods was practised. What is clear, however, is that the sharing of material goods was universally taught and practised by the church into the third century:

All things are common, and the rich are not to be avaricious . . . And it is not right for one to live in luxury, while many are in want. How much more glorious is it to do good to many than to live sumptuously! How much wiser to spend money on human beings than on jewels (Clement of Alexandria, circa AD 200, *Instruction II*, xiii.20.6).

Let the strong take care of the weak; let the weak respect the strong. Let the rich man minister to the poor man; let the poor man give thanks to God that he gave him one through whom his needs might be satisfied (Clement of Rome, circa AD 100, 38:2).

These contributions [that is, put into the church's treasury] are the trust funds of piety. They are not spent on banquets, drinking parties or dining clubs; but for feeding and burying the poor, for boys and girls destitute of property and parents; and further for old people confined to the house, and victims of shipwreck; and any who are in mines, who are exiles to an island, or who are in prison merely on account of God's church – these become the wards of their confession. So great a work of love burns a brand upon us in regard to some. 'See,' they say, 'how they love one another' (Tertullian, circa AD 200, *Apology XXXIX*, 5–11).

Love Feasts

Another important way in which mutual love and care was expressed in the early church was by means of the love feast (or *agape* meal, as it is also called).

The love feast was an integral part of the church's corporate life. Celebrated daily in apostolic times, and then weekly in later years, it consisted of a communal meal to which all were invited. Unlike the majority of modern-day 'services', the pattern of service in the early church consisted of a love feast followed by preaching and then the Eucharist. Just as the disciples and Jesus had shared the Passover meal *before* they shared the bread and wine, so the early church enjoyed an *agape* meal together *before* sharing Communion.

The love feast served two important functions. Not only did it build up the body in an act of mutual sharing and fellowship but crucially it also ensured that the poorer members were able to enjoy a nutritious meal at least once a week. Each person brought along whatever food they had in order to share it with the others. No matter how little some of the poorer members contributed, they were free to help themselves to what the richer members provided. Portions were also sent to the sick and housebound. This was Paul's vision of economic *koinonia* – the rich man voluntarily supplying the poor man's needs that equality might ensue. It was a practice that recalled the way in which manna was to be shared amongst the Israelites in the desert (Ex. 16:14–18) but, thanks to the enabling of the Spirit, it was motivated by love not compulsion:

To that feast everyone brought something, just as he was able. They pooled everything that was brought and then they sat down to share it out together. At this feast all kinds of people were sitting together. Many of the early Christians were very poor; some of them were slaves. A slave's rations in Greece were a quart of meal a day with a few figs and olives and a little wine vinegar. Very often this common meal on the Lord's Day was the only decent meal the slave got all week, and he only got it because in that early Church everyone shared with everyone else everything he had. If the spirit of Christ is really in us we will not be able to be happy if we see someone else in need and do not help him (William Barclay, *God's Young Church*).

Our feast explains itself by its name. The Greeks call it agape, i.e. affection. Whatever it costs, our outlay in the name of piety is gain, since with the good things of the feast we benefit the needy (Tertullian, *Apology XXXIX*, 16).

Unfortunately, the love feast as an integral part of the church's service was short-lived. In the period following Paul's death, worship gradually became more formal and love feasts became detached from the rest of the Sunday service. Holy Communion became the focal point of the church's corporate life. Love feasts continued to be celebrated for a time, but in the evening, as a separate activity from the morning service. However, the same abuses that Paul had written of in 1 Corinthians 11:20–22 (drunkenness, greed, disorder) led to their eventual extinction.

By the end of the third century, the church had travelled a long way from its early, informal origins although some scholars argue this was not universal. A growing distinction was appearing between the role of the clergy and the laity. Churches had begun to acquire property. Not only was the celebration of the love feast detached from the celebration of the Holy Communion, but the latter had become increasingly stylised. The church was becoming ever more institutional in nature and this trend was set to continue, but in a new and totally unforeseen way.

Constantine's Conversion

One of the significant features of early Christianity was that it was an underground movement. Christianity was illegal in the Roman Empire, and those who embraced it were subject to intense persecution. Many lost their lives. One of the most famous stories from the period is that of Polycarp, the Bishop of Smyrna (AD 69–155). Refusing to offer incense on an altar to Caesar, and refusing to call him 'God', he was tied to a stake and set alight. His executioners urged him one last time to save his life by confessing Caesar's divinity, but Polycarp replied: 'Eighty and six years have I served him, and he has done me no wrong. How then can I blaspheme my King and Saviour?'

Such noble acts of martyrdom were not uncommon during the first three centuries of Christianity, but everything changed in the fourth century when Constantine the Great, Emperor of Rome (AD 306–337), converted to Christianity. Suddenly Christians were in the mainstream. Having once been denied freedom to worship, by the end of the fourth century Christianity was not only legal but had been pronounced the official religion of the Empire. The effect on the church was profound.

Whereas once the church had been counter-cultural, now it was very much of its culture. The church and the State became deeply intertwined. The Pope was granted new political authority and Constantine conferred upon himself considerable theological authority. Government money was used to build elaborate church buildings and to subsidise the clergy. Rich landowners built churches for those living on their estates and appointed clergy to manage them. Those who had not been baptised were obliged by imperial law to undergo a course of instruction on the importance of this rite. Those who still refused to get baptised were severely punished. In such a coercive environment, nominalism inevitably flourished. 'Church' came to mean the building rather than the body. People attended rather than belonged. Total commitment was no longer necessary to be a Christian. For many, it was simply a question of expediency.

The question of maintenance started to emerge. How were all of these church buildings going to be maintained? What about the land that the church now owned and what about the clergy?

> By the end of the fifth century the church at Rome had devised a system by which all income from rents and offerings was divided into four parts – for bishop, clergy, the poor, and for repair and lighting of the churches. Elsewhere the distribution varied. Under this system the bishop received an income much greater than that of the priests and deacons – though he had to spend a considerable amount on hospitality. Another contrast was that between rich and poor churches. The wealth of the Roman bishop was enough to make the great pagan senator Praetextatus say, 'Make me a bishop of Rome and I will become a Christian tomorrow.' The regular income of some country clergy was so small, on the other hand, that they had to rely primarily on the generosity of the Christians of their congregation (Jonathan Hill, *The History of Christianity*).

The disciple's practice of the common purse, the Jerusalem church's economic sharing and Paul's preaching about economic *koinonia* were forgotten or, worse, deliberately overlooked. Some churches had plenty, and others were hard pressed. Furthermore, many of the new converts had great riches but they were not being challenged to share them. The radical approach to wealth of the pre-Constantine churches was being replaced by something far less demanding. In his book *Beyond Tithing*, Stuart Murray sums up the changes that were taking place:

Theologians raided the Old Testament and various secular philosophies to develop a new system that would be acceptable in a much broader church. Among the main components of this system were:

- It was no longer a person's actual wealth that mattered but their attitude towards it: wealth could be retained provided one did not feel bound by it;
- Giving was no longer motivated primarily by concern for the poor but by a concern about one's own soul; the spiritual rewards available to givers were emphasised over the material needs of recipients;
- Giving to others was presented as a good investment: what had previously meant living more simply was now seen as likely to result in God increasing one's wealth;
- The concept of *koinonia* was replaced by the concept of 'alms giving' and care for the poor was now regarded as an expression of 'charity' rather than justice;
- The maintenance of church buildings and providing appropriate financial support for church leaders took precedence: anything left over could still be given to the poor;
- Some church leaders began to advocate tithing.

There had been accommodating elements within the church even before Constantine's era. In the middle of the third century, Cyprian, Bishop of Carthage, had pondered in his writings whether tithing should be reintroduced. But it was Constantine's conversion and the ensuing enmeshment of the church and the State that entailed an inexorable trend towards conventional attitudes, one that was embraced by the many and resisted by the few. Theologians and church leaders began to refer back (and selectively at that!) to the Old Testament model of tithing for their teaching on giving. It was a return to the Law, albeit a watered down version. The New Testament witness – what happened at

Pentecost, Paul's vision of economic sharing – was gradually abandoned.

Initially commended as a voluntary offering, tithing was eventually made compulsory across much of Christendom by means of civil legislation. As the church came to own ever increasing amounts of land, tithing metamorphosed into a form of taxation, a means of ensuring the upkeep and maintenance of the church's property, assets, staff and bureaucratic apparatus. Only in the last century was this tax finally abolished in England (with the Tithe Act of 1936), but its legacy endures to this day. When Christian preachers speak about Christian giving, they tend more often to refer back to the Old Testament model of tithing than to the New Testament model of *koinonia*. And, as with the early State church, how much of that money is channelled into building projects and other infrastructure at the expense of directly meeting peoples' needs?

The tragedy and danger of this approach is not only that it overlooks the witness of the Spirit and takes us back to the Law, but also that it represents a diminished version of the Law! Tithing never stood alone in the Old Testament. It came as part of the Jubilee package, once every three years a tithe of the capital was brought to the town square for distribution to the needy. When Spirit-led *koinonia* was and is abandoned in favour of Old Testament models of giving, the Jubilee element of economic justice is grievously overlooked. Why is this so important? Because there is a crucial difference between tithing and Jubilee. Once again, we turn to Stuart Murray's *Beyond Tithing*:

> Tithing, as a percentage measure, [was] applied equally to everyone, but Jubilee would have markedly different implications for those who were rich and those who were poor. The tithe was concerned with income, whereas Jubilee dealt with capital. By comparison with the social upheaval envisaged by the Jubilee provisions, the tithe involved a fairly minor redistribution of resources in favour of the

Levites and the poor. Tithing, unlike the Jubilee, could not prevent the development of a widening gap between rich and poor.

By itself, tithing does nothing to solve economic injustice. It has a mitigating effect, at best. At worst, it serves to salve the conscience of the giver, shielding him from any real examination of his attitude towards wealth and his neighbour. At worst, it patronises the recipient, keeping him a charitable cause and therefore holding him down rather than raising him up to the status of an equal partner. Today we have churches where poorer members (families even), who may not be able to afford a home of their own, are nonetheless taught about the expectation of the church leaders (and so God!) to tithe their income, perhaps to fund the church buildings. Often this will serve the 'vision' or 'mission' of the church. What it will not often do is be used to help the needier members of the congregation.

If people are to be free to enjoy stewardship of God's creation, they need justice, not charity. In the same way that mercy is better than sacrifice,[2] so justice is better than charity. One springs from love, the other springs from duty. By the end of the fourth century, the church had undergone a massive transformation since its birth at Pentecost. It had seen its numbers grow, its geographical boundaries extend, its status officially sanctioned and its power increase. But at what cost? Did it still have a radical, distinctive approach to economic justice? Was it still acting as 'salt' and 'light' in the world? In the church that was developing post-Constantine, charity and duty seemed to be all that was really expected or required.

---

[2] cf. Hosea 6:6; Matthew 12:7.

8

Jubilee Expressions Throughout Church History

The conversion of the Emperor Constantine marked a seismic shift in the church's attitude towards material wealth and Jubilee practices. Where once believers had been persecuted and economically poor, the adoption of the Christian faith by the Emperor as the religion of the Empire led to the aggrandisement of the church. After all, the most powerful ruler of the most powerful nation on earth could hardly be seen worshipping in tenement houses amongst the poor. The church was given vast estates and built splendid cathedrals under the patronage of the Emperor. The clergy enjoyed the lavish and opulent lifestyle befitting servants of the most powerful Empire on earth. With its vast wealth, the church was frankly embarrassed by any reminder of Jubilee practices. Even the teaching called 'the poverty of Christ' (maintaining that Jesus and his disciples were poor) was condemned as a heresy. It is interesting to note that this is a line also effectively taken by many proponents of prosperity teaching today, some of whom maintain, without ground, that Joseph would have been a successful carpenter-businessman, and that Jesus, following in his footsteps would also have been. In reality, the sacrifice that Joseph and Mary brought to the temple at the presentation of Jesus (Lk. 2:24) was that required of poorer members of Israel (Lev. 12:8). The famous story of Thomas

Aquinas illustrates the embarrassment. Whilst being shown around the splendid gold covered cathedrals of Rome, the Pope had said that the church can no longer, like Peter, say 'silver and gold have I do not have' (Acts 3:6). To which Aquinas replied, 'Neither can it say, in the name of Jesus Christ of Nazareth, rise up and walk.'

By the end of the fourth century, the die had firmly been cast. The church had undergone a massive transformation since its birth at Pentecost. It had seen its numbers grow, its geographical boundaries extend, its status officially sanctioned and its power increase. But at what cost? Did it still have a radical, distinctive approach to economic justice?

It was a question that would trouble many over the ensuing years of church history. Whenever sin or complacency set in amongst the majority, there would always be one or two voices in the wilderness calling the church back to its original passion and purity. In this chapter, we are going to spotlight some of the movements and individuals that have emerged over the course of church history to challenge the church about its Jubilee witness. God did not leave himself without any witnesses throughout the centuries. These radical groups sought to express Jubilee in their own distinctive ways. Some were ascetics, others were plainly insular. But each group sought to live simple lives in communities where there was social holiness created through some form of economic sharing. A more detailed description of these radical groups can be found in an earlier book *Lost Heritage*.

Monastic Movements

Although monasticism had existed before Constantine's conversion (St Anthony, circa AD 251–356, is generally considered to be the forefather of the movement), communal monasticism was initiated in about AD 320 by Pachomius in Egypt. Pachomius' approach was less extreme than that of some of his hermetic contemporaries who practised severe forms of self-mortification. Those entering Pachomius' communities surrendered their personal wealth to a common fund. The monks lived a simple, balanced life, without luxuries but also without any harsh deprivations. They had regular meals, regular devotions and regular work periods. The community sought to be self-supporting through such activities as basket weaving and market gardening. As well as supporting themselves, the money they earned was given to the poor and others in need.

Pachomius established a pattern of communal monastic life that many subsequent religious orders would use as the basis of their rule. During the subsequent history of the church, these orders were often important in highlighting the apathy or excesses of the established church. By the early twelfth century, however, this prophetic role had begun to wane. Over the years, many of the orders had accumulated vast amounts of land and property. The monks were therefore spending increasing amounts of time managing their estates.

The Franciscans

It was at this point that an Italian by the name of Francesco di Pietro emerged onto the scene. Just as monasticism appeared to have lost its cutting edge, the Franciscan order appeared, providing perhaps the best example of the monastic tradition's ability to challenge the worldliness endemic in the church. Ironically, though, it was never Francis' ambition to found a religious order. His desire was merely to live out a radical understanding of Christian brotherhood, and to challenge others to do the same. With such an attractive faith as Francis', however, it was not long before his band of brothers had become so large that it became necessary to protect the unity and purity of the community by adopting a rule.

Francis' approach to wealth and possessions was uncompromising. Whereas other orders owned property from which they derived a substantial income, Francis was adamant that his brotherhood would pursue a different path. His brothers would be free spirits, unhampered by material concerns:

> The brothers shall not acquire anything as their own, neither a house nor a place nor anything at all. Instead, as pilgrims and strangers in this world who serve the Lord in poverty and humility, let them go begging for alms with full trust. Nor should they feel ashamed since the Lord made himself poor for us in this world. That is the summit of highest poverty which has established you, my most beloved brothers, as heirs and kings of the kingdom of heaven; it has made you poor in the things of this world but exalted you in virtue. Let this be your portion, which leads into the land of the living. Dedicating yourselves totally to this, my most beloved brothers, do not wish to have anything else for ever under heaven for the sake of our Lord Jesus Christ.
>
> And wherever the brothers may be together or meet other brothers, let them give witness that they are members of one family. And let each one confidently make known his need to the others, for, if a mother has such care and love for her son born according to the flesh, should not someone love and care for his brother according to the Spirit even more diligently? And if any of them becomes sick, the other brothers should serve him as they would wish to be served themselves (Rule 6 from *The Rule of the Friars Minor*, 1223).

Francis understood the corrosive effect that riches could have on the human soul, and he wanted his brothers to be free from their power. In his original Rule of 1210–1221, Francis warned that 'The devil will blind the eyes of those who desire and appreciate money more than stones. Let us take care, we who have left everything, lest for so small a thing we lose the kingdom of heaven.'[1] Material goods were not in themselves bad, but one had to avoid

---

[1] Rule 8 from *The Rule of the Friars Minor*, 1210–1221.

becoming unduly attached to them. Having very little in the first place helped to limit any such attachment, but one also had to be willing to surrender the little one had in the face of another's greater need:

> Francis maintained that for a brother not to part with whatever he had to someone poorer was tantamount to stealing from him or her – a harsh ruling for the friars who had virtually nothing to give except whatever food they had collected and their cloaks. Cloaks feature in a number of anecdotes – to the despair of the brothers who found it difficult to keep warm clothes on Francis' back during hard weather (Adrian House, *Francis of Assisi*).

But Francis' approach to poverty was not primarily built on a negative – the sinfulness of greed, the fear of losing one's soul. It was more fundamentally centred on a positive – the beauty of simplicity, the joy of dependence on God. Because Francis' heart and mind were uncluttered by material worries, he was free to enjoy the gift of God's creation to the full. Like the Celtic saints before him, Francis had a rare synergy with creation. All of God's created beings were Francis' brothers and sisters, and he referred to them as such – the sun, for example, was 'brother sun', and the water was 'sister water'.[2] Whilst we might consider Francis' language amusingly eccentric or, worse, redolent of pantheist spirituality, it was actually rooted in a sound theology of the stewardship of creation and the created order. It was wonderfully consistent with Jubilee values.

We must not make the mistake, then, of reducing Francis to some kind of harmless nature lover. He was far more dangerous than that. The life he lived and the words he preached were deeply challenging to the prevailing culture of the period, both

---

[2] 'The Canticle of the Sun' is St Francis' most famous composition in praise of creation.

within society as a whole and within the church. They are also deeply challenging to our modern-day culture. In our current era of profit-driven industries and economies, debt slavery and intensive farming, materialism yet disconnectedness from the world, we would do well to reflect on the message of St Francis.

Sadly, the Franciscan Order, as so many other religious orders before it, saw its original fervour and influence decline in the years following its founder's death. Following years of internal conflict, and under pressure from the papacy, the Franciscans eventually became property owners. It was a significant development, particularly striking for the way that it exposed the corruption of the papacy.

> In general the Franciscans accepted that poverty was an ideal practised by Christ and the apostles. From this arose the idea that the church hierarchy should remain aloof from entanglements in the world. If extended to the papacy, this put in question the position of the pope as ruler of the princes of Christendom. In addition, the massive wealth of the church as a whole came under scrutiny (Jonathan Hill, *The History of Christianity*).

The Waldensians

A figure contemporaneous with Francis, and just as radical, was a man by the name of Peter Waldo (or Valdes), a merchant from Lyon in France (1140–1218). Much less is known about Waldo or the early Waldensians than is known about Francis or the early Franciscans, but the little that is known reveals some striking similarities.

Like Francis, Waldo's conversion led him to exchange a life of wealth and privilege for one of poverty and simplicity. Like Francis, he was appalled by the excesses of the Pope and other senior members of the Roman Catholic church, and sought to present an alternative based on the example of Jesus. Like the Franciscans, the Waldensians lived an itinerant lifestyle:

They have no fixed habitations. They go about two by two, bare-
foot, clad in woollen garments, owning nothing, holding all things
in common, like the apostles, naked, following a naked Christ
(Walter Map, *De Nugis Curialium*).

It was a lifestyle that embarrassed and riled the papacy. It threw
their profligacy into sharp relief. What's more, Waldo made it his
aim to translate the Gospels from Latin to French, making the
Word of God more accessible to the masses. With this work complete, Waldo and his followers were able to empower people to
understand and embrace the gospel message for themselves.
They were also able to justify their lifestyle as being more genuinely apostolic than that of the Pope and his consorts.

Ordered by the Archbishop of Lyon to stop preaching, the
Waldensians continued regardless. Eventually their refusal to
recognise the authority of the church led to their excommunica-
tion. Their subsequent persecution – many were burnt at the
stake during the Inquisition – failed both to eliminate them and
to prevent their numbers increasing. The movement spread to
other European countries where many thousands were killed or
imprisoned.

Although the orthodoxy of some of the Waldensians' beliefs
may have been questionable, their passion for truth and simplicity had prophetic power, exposing the hypocrisy and complacency of the established church and capturing the hearts and
minds of those who longed for something more authentic than
the institutionalised religious practices of the day.

The Anabaptists

The term Anabaptist is a generic term, denoting a variety of
groups that emerged in Europe (originally Switzerland and
Germany) in the sixteenth century with a vision for renewing
the church. Although in many ways quite diverse, these groups

were united in their rejection of infant baptism, believing that a person's baptism should be accompanied by their confession of faith. It was this belief that led others to call them Anabaptists – literally 'Re-baptisers' – as a term of abuse. But baptism was not, in actual fact, the Anabaptists' primary concern. What troubled them most was the fact that the church had strayed such a long way from its origins. It was not functioning as a body, but as a complex hierarchical institution. Moreover, it had compromised its integrity by its accumulation of great wealth and its dependence on the State. The Anabaptists longed to restore to the church its original purity, simplicity and fervour.

As well as being persecuted by the Roman Catholics and the Protestants, the Anabaptists were denounced by leaders of the Reformation such as Luther and Zwingli. One of the things that the Reformers disliked about them was that they qualified the principle of justification by faith by emphasising the importance of works of righteousness. They insisted on a radical lifestyle of mutual love and service. They were committed to economic justice and wealth redistribution and saw this as one of their distinguishing characteristics:

> Is it not sad and intolerable hypocrisy that these poor people [the Lutherans] boast of having the Word of God, of being the true, Christian church, never remembering that they have entirely lost their sign of true Christianity. For although many of them have plenty of everything, go about in silk and velvet, gold and silver, and in all manner of pomp and splendour; ornament their houses with all manner of costly furniture; have their coffers filled, and live in luxury and splendour, yet they suffer many of their own poor, afflicted members (notwithstanding their fellow believers who have received one baptism and partaken of the same bread with them) to ask for alms; and poor, hungry, suffering, old, lame, blind, and sick people to beg their

bread at their doors' ('Reply to False Accusations', Menno Simons, 1552).

The Anabaptists were widely regarded as subversive and rebellious. One of their core beliefs, that the church should be separated from the State, threatened to rock the very foundations of society. They had to be quashed. Approximately 2,500 were executed – half the number of all Christians, of whatever confession, killed for their faith during the Reformation – and the majority of those that survived lived a peripatetic existence, constantly on the move to avoid capture.

The Hutterites

Some of the Anabaptists found refuge in Moravia where they were able to settle without threat of persecution. Drawing their inspiration from the early church, in 1529 they formed a community called the Bruderhof based on the principle of economic *koinonia*.

Jacob Wiedemann, one of the original leaders of the Bruderhof, was autocratic and the movement would not have survived but for the efforts of Jacob Hutter (1500–1536). It is a credit to his leadership that these Anabaptists chose to be named after him even though he was not their founder.

Under the able leadership of men such as Peter Walpot (1518–1578) and Peter Riedemann (1506–1566), the Hutterites founded some 100 Bruderhofs with a total membership of 30,000–70,000. Each Bruderhof was a self-sufficient community, where the community of goods was practised. Men and women were assigned to work according to their abilities. Children were cared for in the Bruderhofs' own nurseries and schools. The Hutterites are said to have enjoyed 100 per cent literacy, a remarkable achievement for that time and place.

The Hutterites' lifestyle provided a living testimony of the biblical principle that the pooling of resources works to everyone's advantage. It is not something that the wealthier members should fear, as if only the poor will benefit.[3] Thanks to their communal approach to wealth, goods and talents, the Hutterite brothers prospered economically as well as educationally. It is a pattern of success that endures to this day:

> Today there are nearly 400 colonies of the Hutterian Brethren in Canada and the United States and a few more in South America and Europe. When a Hutterian community reaches its optimum capacity (100–150 members), the group acquires a new piece of land, builds a new set of structures (homes, barns, schools etc.), acquires more agricultural equipment, and outfits an entire new facility. Then the population divides into two groups – one group staying at the original site, and one moving on to the new one. Neighboring colonies support each other with backup labor and various resources, an approach that yields a very high ratio of success for the new colonies.
>
> Each colony has common work and a common purpose, and most have an economic base of large-scale, machine-powered agriculture within an organizational structure resembling that of a producer cooperative. Because the Hutterites have retained many of their original customs – including dress, family structure, a

---

[3] This, of course, is one of the fears of the world's richest countries today. If they cancel the debts of the poorer countries, will they themselves not be worse off? In fact, leading economists suggest that the opposite is true. Promoting the welfare of another, be it an individual or a nation, leads to an improvement in one's own welfare. (For further study on this subject, an excellent resource is *The End of Poverty: How We Can Make It Happen In Our Lifetime* by Jeffrey Sachs.) The biblical message on this point corroborates the economic facts. Wealth held onto does not bless the hoarder, it becomes a liability (Exodus 16:20, James 5:2,3). On the other hand, the wealthy will not go without if they share (Malachi 3:10–12, Luke 6:38). Despite sharing what he had with a crowd of 5,000, the boy with five loaves and two fishes still 'had enough to eat' himself (John 6:12,13).

simple lifestyle, and the German language – many outsiders find the Hutterites to be quite out of place when compared to their contemporary neighbors. Yet they have been so successful in their endeavors that in the '80s some of their neighbors on the Canadian plains initiated lawsuits to prevent Hutterites from acquiring more land, claiming that their modernized agricultural base and communal economy amounted to 'unfair competition' (Geoph Kozeny, 'Intentional Communities: Lifestyles Based on Ideals', *1999 Communities Directory*, Fellowship for Intentional Community).

One of the reasons these radical groups were persecuted was because their lifestyles were a direct challenge to the established church at that time. By and large, those who sought to live Jubilee lifestyles did so as deviants. Prolonged persecution and isolation can create eccentricities. Whatever their quirkiness, above all, these communities were characterised by social holiness, brotherhood (or 'family') and economic sharing. For many, their understanding of Jubilee *shalom* extended also to being pacifists, many of them choosing to follow the teachings of Jesus regarding enemy-loving.

9

Modern Expressions of Jubilee

Clearly our economic situation is very different from the time of Moses and the giving of the Jubilee laws. Most of us are not farmers owning our own plots of land. But as we have seen through the centuries since Pentecost, many groups have sought to be faithful to the spirit of Jubilee, often paying a price for their faithfulness. At each stage, however, these groups emphasised different Jubilee principles as determined by their environment. Some sought to embrace all the Jubilee practices of the Jerusalem church. Others expressed what they could. But all were seeking to express Jubilee generosity and social holiness.

We now turn to how we today might imitate these groups to express Jubilee in similarly varied ways appropriate to our economic environment.

Community Living

In 1979 a group of students from Surrey University, UK started living in community. I was one of them. At its peak, there were about forty of us living in about twelve houses, most of which we owned. In line with our understanding of private ownership and Jubilee, we assisted each other to buy our own houses. We gifted each other with sums of money for the deposit so that the balance could be financed through a mortgage. We did not have a trust or a centralised holding entity for these properties, having seen how centralisation of ownership had affected the monastic movement. All our houses were privately owned. This community lasted for eight years. For us community was not an end in itself. We saw it as an environment where discipleship could take place. It was an environment for God to deal with our material addiction. We shared our material wealth (the little that we had) with our extended family and friends. Surplus financial resources were released to help others. For us it was also a time of intense study of the Bible and everyone amassed a library of reference books. We paraphrased Tertullian by saying that we had all things in common among us except our wives and our books! (Christians are pretty bad at returning books.) Throughout this time, we were not a church but remained members of several different churches. Over time, some took up leadership in their churches but the time commitment to church, career, young family and community eventually led us to 'disband' so that we could commit ourselves to our churches. Post-community, some of us still live as extended families where single people have lived with us without rent (they are family after all) in order that they might save towards getting married or a deposit for a house (particularly relevant in countries with house price inflation).

Another example is the Bugbrooke Community, UK started in the 1970s and now called the Jesus Army. It remains one of the most dynamic and radical communities I know. It has a centralised ownership of property and owns hundreds of acres of farm land where organic food is produced. Apart from farming, the community runs a number of other businesses including food wholesaling, house building and restoration. The community has a great work amongst the marginalised and disadvantaged who are brought to the community to live and work on the farms and other businesses as part of their rehabilitation from mental illness, criminal activities and substance abuse. One can safely say, 'there was and are no poor among them'.

We are not all called to live in community of this sort, whether in cities (as we did) or in villages, as the Bugbrooke Community still do. But clearly it is the most holistic of environments where the extended family is a reality, love is practical, the poor and needy are cared for, material addiction is curbed. There is *shalom* – wholesomeness.

Distribution of Wealth

In the venture capital world, share option is an important way to incentivise staff performance. Great wealth has been created by the technology and biotechnology booms and these have also resulted in some of that wealth being distributed to employees through share options.

In all the businesses that I have been involved with, I have sought to practice a distribution of wealth. Such distributions have been used for a variety of things including paying off mortgages and securing pensions for missionaries. When I asked my fellow directors in one of my businesses in Asia to structure a share option scheme for our staff, they thought I meant the senior management. When I explained that I believe the cleaners should also be included, they baulked. In the hierarchical society of Asia, cleaners were not deemed important enough to be rewarded. To the credit of my fellow shareholders they agreed and everyone participated in the share option scheme. The majority of the staff had never owned shares in a public company before and had to be taught their responsibilities as shareholders and the mechanics of share trading. I remember a nurse who exercised her options, sold her shares to fund her son's university education in the United States, something she could not have afforded before.

It is clear in the business world today that for many people a salary is not enough. Real empowerment comes through ownership, and share options are a great way to allow staff to share in the success of the company and a way of practising wealth distribution. So to those readers who own businesses, why not proclaim a Jubilee and distribute some of your wealth?

Cancellation of Debt

We can also practice cancellation of debts as private individuals. Remember, cancelling a debt just converts it into a gift. The sermon on the mount encourages us to give rather than lend.

By far the most impressive debt cancellation programme we have ever seen was that initiated by the Jubilee 2000 Movement. This called on the rich countries to cancel the debts of the Highly Indebted Poor Countries. To date US$60 billion of debt from twenty-six countries has been cancelled.

Jubilee in Fremantle, Australia

A group of churches in Fremantle, Perth felt God calling them to proclaim a Jubilee to the people of Fremantle. They raised over A$80,000 and persuaded the utility companies to cancel the debts of those whose electricity, gas and water had been cut off through arrears. On Easter day 2003, the utility companies wrote to their debtors and said that through the generosity of the churches in Fremantle, their debts had been cancelled and their utilities reconnected. Because of the Data Protection Laws, the churches could not have direct contact with the utility customers so the utility companies included a letter from the churches explaining why they were proclaiming a Jubilee with a telephone contact for people who wanted to contact them. This news hit the national television, with the mayor and church leaders being interviewed. Many other acts of generosity were practised throughout the Jubilee Week. Also on the hour, for the whole week, the local radio station announced where families have had their utilities reconnected and the sums of debt cancelled. It was the most popular radio station that week. What an imaginative expression of Jubilee this was. This is the church. This is the kind of church to belong to. It is relevant. It smells of God's justice and compassion for the poor.[1]

Storehouses

During our time in community, we had a converted garden shed that acted as a storehouse. We did our shopping in bulk to reduce costs. Apart from using it for our own needs, food from the storehouse was also used to share with needy students.

Every church should have a storehouse of food, clothes, household goods where the poor can come and take what they need. Indeed, one of the earliest excavations we have of 'house churches' from the second to third centuries, shows a simple structure in the shape of a cross, in three sections – the main auditorium flanked by a 'baptistery' on one side and a storehouse on the other. The separate baptistery was because believers were baptised naked, and the storehouse was to store the offerings brought by the congregation for distribution to poor and needy by the elders. This shows the priority that the church gave towards meeting the needs of the poor. Unfortunately, few of our church buildings today are designed for this.

Food Distribution

Catholic Worker Movement

The Catholic Worker Movement was founded in 1933, in New York, by Dorothy Day and Peter Maurin. The movement started life as a newspaper, the *Catholic Worker*, born out of Dorothy and Peter's frustration with the church and fuelled by their vision to promote Catholic social teaching and action. It was the era of the

---

[1] See www.ausprayernet.org.au/trans_articles4.php and www.fremantleJubilee.asn.au

Great Depression, when many were unemployed and living in conditions of dire poverty. The church's failure to take any meaningful action or stand on these issues had caused many to embrace the Communist cause, believing it to be the only way out of their despair. Dorothy herself had resisted joining the church for many years because of its lukewarm efforts to address the suffering of the masses. What she was looking for was not charity but an approach to the poor that contained 'a strong sense of man's dignity and worth, and what was due to him in justice'.

Focusing chiefly on the needs of 'the poor, the dispossessed, the exploited', the newspaper was not afraid to tackle challenging subjects. One of Peter's major preoccupations was the problem of homelessness and he was inspired by examples from the fifth-century church of 'houses of hospitality', open to the poor, sick, orphaned, elderly, travellers and so on. Sharing his thoughts on the subject in the newspaper, his articles and poems struck a chord in the hearts of many, both those in need and those wanting to help. As winter approached, only six months after the newspaper's first issue had gone out, the homeless came knocking on Dorothy's door. Meanwhile, donations of money, food and clothing flooded in, and volunteers came forward offering their services. The newspaper was metamorphosing organically into a movement, a community of individuals committed, like Dorothy and Peter, to live out a lifestyle based on the values of the Sermon on the Mount. Dorothy's apartment became the first of many houses of hospitality, scattered across the United States, offering unconditional love, acceptance, food and shelter to the poor and downtrodden.

It was the search for economic and social justice that lay at the heart of the Catholic Worker Movement. But the Workers found their inspiration in the gospel, not in any political ideologies of the day, despite the fact that the majority of priests, Dorothy felt, were 'businesslike', and demonstrated a widespread 'lack of a sense of responsibility for the poor'. Believing passionately that 'our salvation depends on the poor' because 'Christ identifies himself' with them, Dorothy was not afraid to challenge the assumptions and prejudices of those who approached the poor with an attitude of pity or superiority. The Workers' standards were to provide the best available coffee and bread for the destitute that visited them. Other acts of radical generosity were part and parcel of their way of life. Although often criticised for such generosity, Dorothy's rationale was simple:

> My radical associates were the ones who were in the forefront of the struggle for a better social order where there would not be so many poor . . . We believe in loving our brothers regardless of race, color or creed and we believe in showing this love by working for better conditions immediately and the ultimate owning by the workers of their means of production. We believe in an economy based on human needs rather than on the profit motive (Robert Ellesberg, Ed., *Dorothy Day: Selected Writings*).

The Catholic Workers not only met individuals at their place of need but also took their message out onto the streets, joining protest marches and labour pickets. Political involvement was as much a part of the movement as acts of mercy. Decrying the inadequate wages and poor working conditions that some companies offered their employees, they urged the public to use the power of boycott in order to bring about change.

Mother Teresa

Originally from Macedonia, Mother Teresa first arrived in Calcutta aged twenty and began teaching in a school of her church order. It was in 1948 that, having been given permission to leave the order, she moved into the poorest parts of Calcutta and set up her own open-air school for children living in the slums. In 1950, she gained approval for a new order, the Missionaries of Charity, whose self-description was to give love and care to those who are unloved and uncared for. In her time Mother Teresa became known as the 'Saint of the Gutters' because of her persistent care and devotion to the poorest people in Calcutta, particularly the dying although also the abused, neglected, diseased and deprived. Providing food for these poor was one of the routine activities of the order. In 1952, she founded the Nirmal Hriday Home for the Dying, providing a distinctive emphasis, in a predominantly Hindu context, on the dignity of human life and the care owed to the terminally ill.

Mother Teresa's order has spread all over the world offering relief in situations of humanitarian crises, such as floods and famines. No one is too poor or in too much suffering to be looked after – alcoholics, sufferers of HIV/AIDS and other epidemics. In 1979, she was awarded the Nobel Peace Prize, just one among several high accolades. Yet it should be noted that for all of the momentum the Missionaries of Charity order gained, and for the countless times Mother Teresa has been held up as a moral example, it all began with just one woman caring for another. As Mother Teresa herself once said: 'Do not wait for leaders; do it alone, person to person.'

Hospitality

Aliens' hospitality programmes are important – I was an alien once in the UK. I know what it was like to be a foreigner and what the Bible teaches about welcoming foreigners is music to my ears. Unfortunately, our churches are not very welcoming and hospitable places. Friends International is a great organisation working with overseas students. My wife and a number of other ladies run one of their hospitality programmes. Over the years, we have had hundreds of overseas students in our house (and garden). What a richness these overseas students bring to our understanding of the world and what an opportunity to demonstrate God's love and generosity. If we understand Jubilee, the church should be synonymous with hospitality, and Christians with generosity.

Some churches have meals together after a church service. This follows in the great tradition of the early church with their love feasts. If we extend these meals to the poor, the widows and the aliens, we will be expressing something of the Jubilee.

Shalom

We have seen the vision of *shalom* described as each man sitting outside their own house, under his own vine and fig-tree in the evenings, after a day's work, telling stories. Having a roof over one's head and an opportunity to work is a part of the Jubilee agenda. Helping the poor with their housing needs is a part of Jubilee. As is helping the poor with employment. Christians in the comfort-driven West often talk about 'being' over and against 'doing', 'after all,' they say, 'we're human *beings* not human *doings*'. Yet a biblical worldview affirms that God made us to work, to be doers. 'Doing' what God has created us to do is part of what makes us human. It's part of having a God-given dominion over the earth. We are hard-wired to fulfil our potential and so the idea that we can experience a state of *shalom* before God irrespective of what we do with our lives is a fallacy. If our understanding is that God had put man to work in the garden, the absence of work (unemployment) should become for us a mission issue. Our experience is that when the long-term unemployed are offered permanent employment, their whole personality changes, their spirit lifted. I see in this something of God's image being restored in these people. The weary and heavy-laden have been offered *shabbat* rest (just not in the narrow sense as it's so often understood today).

Treasury Fund

Some churches (many Mennonites) still practise the common purse or treasury fund of the early church. This is a fund set aside for the poor and to be disbursed by the leaders of the church for the needy. Every church should have a Jubilee Fund to meet the needs of its own members but beyond that, to help those in an emergency. The Citizens Advice Bureau (CAB) is a wonderful legal-aid organisation funded by the British government but staffed mainly by highly trained volunteers. It deals with all kinds of problems of ordinary citizens with housing, debt and quasi-legal needs. During an emergency, cases may be referred to a group of lawyers in town who have an emergency fund to tide people over until they can be properly sorted out. Where is the church in this? Should not the church be *the* natural refuge for the needy? It certainly was in the first three centuries. And in Old Testament times, the poor would have been cared for by the structure that God had instituted before people dismantled and destroyed it by becoming like the other nations.

At the Millmead church, Guildford, when the offering bag was passed around, I remember the pastor, David Pawson encouraging those who had needs to take from the bag rather than putting money in. This was a great gesture, but in a very public setting I don't know if anyone ever did. Yet the motives were clear – if we are truly family, we should look after each other's needs.

So where does all this leave us? When the Spirit comes he brings Jubilee – he creates community, a sense of belonging, of family. Cold, unwelcoming churches are not communities, whatever they call themselves. Neither are churches that do not care for their poorer members and non-members. Jubilee challenges us to love our neighbours in a world of inequalities. And as we have seen, there are so many imaginative and simple ways of expressing Jubilee – simple but costly, and only possible through the transforming power of the Spirit. Jubilee generosity and hospitality stand as a witness against our materialistic consumerist society. Jubilee distribution of wealth will help to meet the needs of an unjust world. Jubilee community and belonging addresses the loneliness of our age. Jubilee *shalom* is a powerful antidote to a society propped up by Valium.

> The LORD is my shepherd, I shall not be in want.
> He makes me lie down in green pastures,
> he leads me beside quiet waters,
>> he restores my soul.
> He guides me in paths of righteousness for his name's sake . . .
> Surely goodness and love [mercy] will follow me all the days of
>> my life,
> and I will dwell in the house of the LORD for ever (Psalm 23).
> *Shalom*

Bibliography

(listing most recent editions)

Barclay, William, *God's Young Church: A Study of the Early Church* (Edinburgh: Saint Andrew Press, 1991).

Brueggemann, Walter, *A Social Reading of the Old Testament: Prophetic Approaches to Israel's Communal Life* (Minneapolis, MN: Augsburg Fortress, 1994).

De Vaux, Roland, *Ancient Israel: Its Life and Institutions* (Grand Rapids, MI: William B. Eerdmans Publishing Co., 1997).

Ellsberg, Robert (Ed.), *Dorothy Day: Selected Writings* (Maryknoll, NY: Orbis Books, 1992).

Ellul, Jacques, *Money and Power* (Nottingham: InterVarsity Press, 1984).

Foster, Richard, *Money, Sex and Power: The Challenge of the Disciplined Life* (London: Hodder & Stoughton, 1999, new edition).

Gill, Anthony, 'State Welfare Spending and Religiosity' (*Rationality and Society*, Vol. 16, No. 4, Sage Publications, 2004).

Green, Joel, *The Theology of the Gospel of Luke* (Cambridge: Cambridge University Press, 1995).

Heaton, Eric William, *The Hebrew Kingdoms* (Oxford: Oxford University Press, 1981).

Hill, Jonathan, *The New Lion Handbook: The History of Christianity* (Oxford: Lion Hudson, 2007).

House, Adrian, *Francis of Assisi: A Revolutionary Life* (Mahwah, NJ: Paulist Press, 2003).

Jeremias, Joachim, *New Testament Theology. Volume One: The Proclamation of Jesus* (London: SCM Press, 1971).

Kreider, Alan, *Journey Towards Holiness: A Way of Living for God's Nation* (Scottdale, PA: Herald Press, 1987).

Marshall, I. Howard, *The Gospel of Luke: A Commentary on the Greek Text* (Milton Keynes: Paternoster, 1978).

Murray, Stuart, *Beyond Tithing* (Milton Keynes: Paternoster, 2002).

Murray, Stuart, *Post-Christendom: Church and Mission in a Strange New World* (Milton Keynes: Paternoster, 2004).

Myers, Ched, *Jesus' New Economy of Grace, Sojourners 27*, no. 4 (Washington, DC: 1998), 36–39.

Newbigin, Lesslie, *The Household of God* (London: SCM Press, 1953).

Stark, Rodney, *The Rise of Christianity: How the Obscure, Marginal Jesus Movement became the Dominant Religious Force in the Western World in a Few Centuries* (Princeton, NJ: Princeton University Press, 1996).

Wright, Christopher J.H., *Old Testament Ethics for the People of God* (Nottingham: InterVarsity Press, 2004).

Yoder, John Howard, *The Politics of Jesus* (Grand Rapids, MI: William B. Eerdmans Publishing Co., 1996, second edition).

Other Books by the Author

Lost Heritage: The Story of Radical Christianity (Godalming: Highland Books, 1996).

Sting in the Tail: The Parables as Oriental Stories (with Rima Minassian) (Normandy: Bethel Books, 1998, reprinted 2006).

Understanding the Bible through Eastern Eyes (Normandy: Bethel Books, 2001).

Fighting Poverty Through Enterprise (with Lord Brian Griffiths) (London: Transformational Business Network, 2007).

CM 8 + 9